To the Bestest

On farther's day   World
2006

# BRAIN
# FITNESS
# @WORK

From the greatest little
boy

hamlyn

# BRAIN
# FITNESS
# @WORK

Judith Jewell

First published in Great Britain in 2003 by
Hamlyn, a division of Octopus Publishing Group Ltd
2–4 Heron Quays, London E14 4JP

ISBN 0 600 60721 6

A CIP catalogue record for this book is available from
the British Library


Printed and bound in Italy

10 9 8 7 6 5 4 3 2 1

# CONTENTS

# INTRODUCTION

Why do some people always seem to be full of clever ideas? Why are some people able to 'think on their feet'? Why are other people always first to remember what was said at last month's meeting?

Were they simply born smarter, quicker and more alert than the rest of us? Or could it be that they have realized that brains are like every other part of our bodies – and can be exercised and stretched and improved?

Like most people, I spent many years without thinking about how my brain worked. I just got on with school, college, and then work, assuming that sometimes I would come up with ideas – and sometimes I wouldn't. I knew I was quite creative – people told me my drawing was good and I got good marks for some of my poems – and I scored well in maths and science, most of the time. But I do not recall ever being taught how to get the best out of my brain, or how to sharpen up my multiple intelligences, or how to maximize my memory.

Science is providing more answers, and generating even more questions about the way our minds and memories work. We are now becoming more aware that creativity isn't confined to traditional areas. In addition, people are less willing to be judged solely on academic achievement.

## *Our brains have vast potential – we need a way to unlock it*

This book is the result of many years experience of using my brain at work as a management consultant, and twenty years of education before that. It is the product of all that I have read and learned and found out. It reflects stories and experiences from my own life and those of others who have shared their experiences with me. Where I have drawn directly on others' work I have aimed to acknowledge it. But the sources of some of the ideas that my mind has provided me with are unacknowledged because I simply do not recall how I came by them. All I can do is thank the anonymous donors and hope that I have done those ideas justice.

**This book is for *you* if ...**

You have ever wondered why ... **you sometimes forget important things**

... **your best ideas come *after* the meeting**

... **you see things so differently from your colleagues**

You would like to improve ... **your resistance to distractions**

... **your ability to solve problems**

... **the way your meetings run**

You want to find out ... **all the different ways you are intelligent**

... **how you can heighten your five senses**

... **how to make sure you always communicate clearly**

You enjoy ... **looking at things in new ways**

... **questionnaires that tell you about yourself**

... **stretching your mind**

# WARM-UP
## EXERCISES

Try these exercises to get your brain limbered up. (The answers are on page 138):

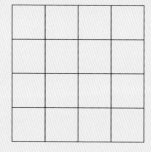

◀ **1**  How many squares are there in this picture?

**2**  What comes next in this sequence?

**3  4  6  8  12  14**

**3**  The answers to these clues are words which sound alike but are spelled differently.
For example, FRUIT and TWO – PEAR and PAIR

| | |
|---|---|
| **GOLF ACCESSORY** | **PROHIBITED** |
| **DRINK** | **GROUP OF MUSICIANS** |
| **NUMBER** | **MAN** |
| **ALSO** | **POST** |
| **COMPLETE** | **CONCEITED** |
| **PERFORATION** | **BLOOD VESSEL** |
| **PART OF A PLAY** | **ROUGHLY STITCHED** |
| **NOTICED** | **DIPLOMACY** |

*(handwritten: 2  TOO next to NUMBER / ALSO)*

◀ **4**  What is the lowest number of coins you need to move to get the triangle pointing downwards?

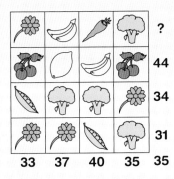

| | | | | ? |
|---|---|---|---|---|
| | | | | 44 |
| | | | | 34 |
| | | | | 31 |
| 33 | 37 | 40 | 35 | 35 |

**◄ 5** Fill in the missing number:

**6** Which two letters belong in the gap?

| | | |
|---|---|---|
| CN | LF | PV |
| DP | ?? | QX |
| ER | NJ | RZ |

**7** Each of three friends – Mr Carpenter, Mr Mason and Mr Painter – is engaged in a different occupation. By a strange coincidence, one is a carpenter, one is a mason and one a painter; but their names do not necessarily match their trades.

Assuming that only one of the following statements is true, who does what?

**Mr Carpenter is not a painter**
**Mr Mason is not a carpenter**
**Mr Carpenter is a carpenter**
**Mr Mason is not a painter**

**8** What room does the head of Human Resources work in?

| | |
|---|---|
| **CHIEF EXECUTIVE** | **Room 28** |
| **MARKETING DIRECTOR** | **Room 29** |
| **FINANCE DIRECTOR** | **Room 27** |
| **HEAD OF HR** | **Room ?** |

**9** Continue the sequence by adding H, I and J in the correct places:

A           E F
    B C D       G

**10** Martha has to get her two babies, Roger and Sara, as well as the family cat, out to the car. Because Martha has a broken arm she can only carry one baby or the cat at a time. Unfortunately, neither baby can be left alone with the cat because Sara pulls the cat's tail, causing general chaos, and the cat will shed white fur on Roger's new navy sailor suit. How does she get everyone to the car in as few round trips as possible?

# 1 HOW OUR BRAINS WORK

*'People travel to wonder at the highest of mountains, at the huge waves of the sea, at the long course of rivers, at the vast compass of the ocean, at the circular motion of the stars and they pass by themselves without wondering.' Saint Augustine of Hippo*

The last great frontier – this is how many scientists describe their work on the brain and the mind. Research findings about how our brains work often make the news and yet the experts often seem to disagree about what the results of the research mean.

One thing everyone does agree on though is that our brains are incredibly powerful.

They may only be the size and weight of an ovenready chicken but they enable us to:

• read the newspaper

• hear and understand what the person next to us is saying

• feel excited about our next holiday

• notice the smell of a bacon sandwich and that nagging pain in our shoulder

What's more – we can probably do them all at the same time. This is because our brains can make more connections and patterns of thought than there are atoms in the universe.

# How our brains are constructed

Our brains have evolved over many thousands of years into the complex organs that we now take for granted, and their development can be traced in how the different parts of them function today.

All of the original brain functions we started out with are controlled by what is known as our 'primitive' brain. This region is about the size of an apricot and governs our basic physical functions, like blood circulation, breathing and digestion. It is also responsible for the 'fight or flight' response to danger, which determines whether we will stand up to a threat or run away. Scientists believe that when we are under stress, the other parts of our brain partially shut down and leave everything up to the primitive brain, which is why we can find it hard to think rationally when we feel 'up against it'.

The second part of our brain to develop was our 'mammalian brain' – the part which is also found in most mammals. Physically it sits around the primitive brain and takes charge of processing our emotions and long-term memories. It also processes the information collected through our senses and passes it up the line for decisions to be made.

Covering these two regions is our most advanced brain, the 'cerebral cortex', which makes up about 80 per cent of our brain area. This is the wrinkled covering that we most usually see in a jar in horror movies. It is responsible for complex movement patterns, language, thought, reasoning, and things like appreciation of poetry and music.

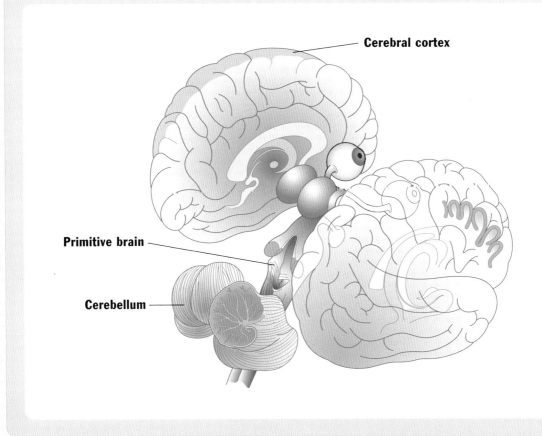

**Cerebral cortex**

**Primitive brain**

**Cerebellum**

# Under the microscope

We all have millions of brain cells, called neurons, and each one is unique with its own special function. They use electrical impulses and chemical reactions to send and receive messages to and from the central nervous system and within the brain itself.

A neuron looks like a fantasy creature from outer space or a piece of plankton. Its central body has feathery arms, called dendrites, which receive and transmit the chemical information from and to other neurons, and translate it into electrical impulses. One longer dendrite – the axon – works like a lightning conductor. It collects all the impulses and sends them, at up to 120 metres (130 yards) per second, to relevant groups of neurons so that the appropriate reaction can happen.

Neurons store information and work together to generate actions and reactions. They work in groups, each controlling specific tasks. Each neuron has the potential for one million billion connections with other neurons – scientists estimate that on average we only use five per cent of our brain capacity in our lifetime.

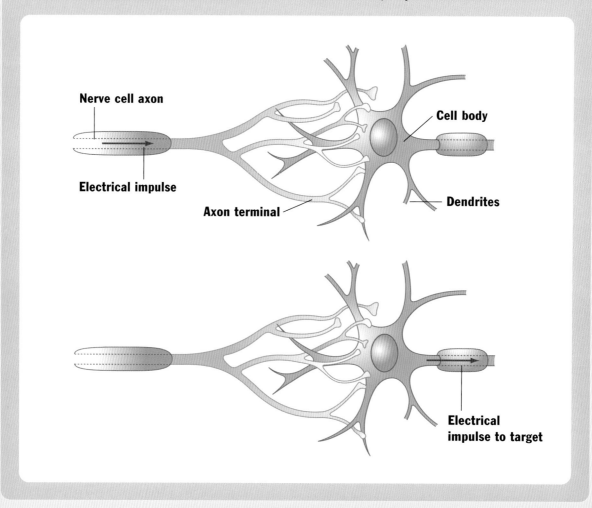

Nerve cell axon

Electrical impulse

Axon terminal

Cell body

Dendrites

Electrical impulse to target

# The left and right hemispheres

For many years people thought that we have two brains, just as we usually have two lungs or two kidneys. As long ago as ancient Egypt, people had noticed that the left side of the brain appeared to control the right side of the body and vice versa. Much more recently, in the 1960s, Roger Sperry (a psychobiologist at the California Institute of Technology) discovered that the two halves of the brain are associated with different activities.

The left side of our brain handles logical issues, and mathematical and sequential processing. It deals with details, organizes data, and controls speech and writing.

The right side operates in a more random, less organized way. It handles creativity, interpretation and metaphor and so on and works with our feelings and our intuition.

At one time, scientists believed the various parts of the brain were entirely separate, but new thinking suggests that they can operate in a more flexible way and that different parts of the brain can learn new functions.

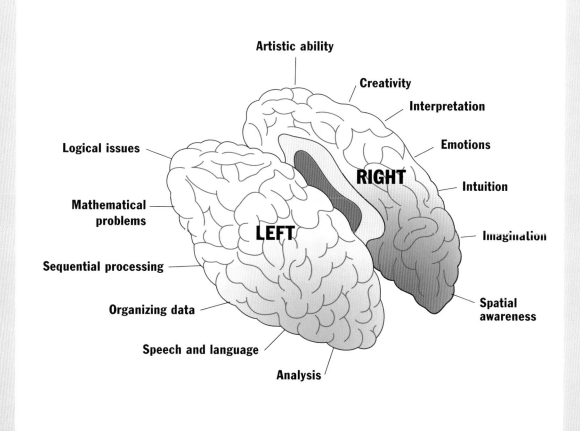

# MAKING SENSE OF
# OUR SENSES

*All day, every day, the world around us bombards us with information. Our five senses –
sight, hearing, touch, smell and taste – pick up the messages that the objects and people
around us are sending out, and our brains process them. And that is where the difficulty lies.
How reliable are our senses?*

The philosopher, René Descartes, noticed that we can be fooled by our senses.
He conducted a simple experiment, which is easy to duplicate. Fill three bowls
with water of different temperatures – one ice cold, one lukewarm and one as
hot as you can stand. Put one hand each into the hot and cold bowls for one
minute then put both in the lukewarm water. Your brain is receiving different
messages about the temperature of this tepid water from each hand: one tells
you that the water is hot, the other that it is cool. Which is correct?

This unusual figure shows the parts of the body as
they appear to the brain. The physical size of each
part is related to the size of the area of the brain
controlling that part's activity.

Even though you know, logically, that the water in the
third bowl is at just one, uniform temperature, what the
messages from your hands are telling you contradicts
this. They are giving messages about the temperature
*relative to* what they have been used to. It's usually
enough to know that something is hot compared to
normal, for example, so that our body can react
accordingly, but our brains have the ability to take this
further. It's one thing for the brain to be able to
recognize that a cup of coffee is hot, but then
experience and assumptions come into play to interpret
that information, enabling you to make a decision
about whether it's so hot that you'll scald yourself if
you drink it.

# How the brain controls the body

When you make any movement, the action starts as a burst of electrical nerve activity in the cerebral cortex. The motor cortex then sends out nerve signals destined for a certain part of the body. Parts which have very fine control, such as the fingers and lips, have bigger patches of motor cortex. The signals emerge from the base of the brain and flash down the spinal cord, out along motor nerves to the muscles. Nerves that carry messages from brain to muscles are motor nerves.

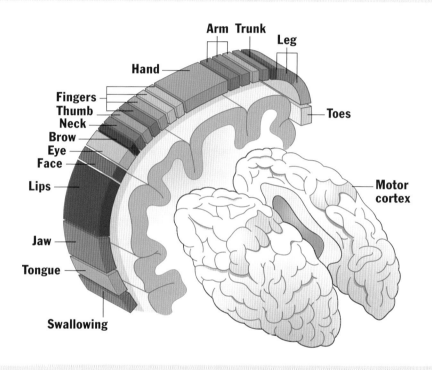

# Personal perceptions

Even assuming all your five senses are intact and working well, what your brain tells you about the world will be different from what someone else would notice and think about a situation or event.

There are myriad opportunities for us to be fooled by our senses and to disagree with co-workers about what's going on. Just think about the last meeting you went to. Perhaps two people got into a discussion about what they thought they heard a senior manager say at a conference. Two other people couldn't agree on whether the room was too hot or not and perhaps you thought that the perfume the person next to you was wearing was rather cloying (they think it's alluring) and as for the taste of the new brand of coffee that the person running the meeting had chosen ...

# UNDERSTANDING AND
## HEIGHTENING YOUR SENSES

*There is good evidence that the more you are able to use your senses the better your memory and thinking abilities will be. The activities below are designed to make you more aware of your senses, so that you can understand what they are telling you more readily.*

## SIGHT

We can distinguish millions of colours, hundreds of shades of brightness, distance, perspective, size, movement and shape, using the 130 million photoreceptors in our eyes. The visual cortex, which takes up 30 per cent of the cortex, is at the back of the head. Different groups of cells are responsible for distinguishing details such as colour, distance, edges and angles. This is why some people with localized brain damage may lose only some aspects of their ability to process images. For example, they may still be able to see the colour and shape of a cup, but not to distinguish how near it is.

### Activity

*Choose an item for visual study. Don't pick it up – just look at something out of the window or at a group of objects on your desk.*
*What colours do you see? Check that you are noticing shades of those colours. What shapes are any shadows making? Imagine turning the object through 90 degrees. What is on its front now? Close each eye in turn. How does this affect the size, shape and colour of your object?*

## HEARING

The structure of our hearing system is simple, ingenious and a marvel of miniaturization. Packed into about 2cm$^3$ are a hydraulic balance system, a sound-wave analyser, a noise-reduction unit, a multi-channel transducer and a relay unit. We have 16,000 hair cells in our inner ear and we lose about 40 per cent by the time we're 65.

When we start to speak, muscles in our middle ear contract to dampen the sound of our own voice and incoming low-level frequencies. If this didn't happen, we wouldn't be able to talk and listen at the same time.

### Activity

*Spend two minutes listening. Notice all the sounds close to you. Separate them out in your mind. Which are loud and which soft? Then gradually bring in sounds from a wider radius. Try to listen to them above the nearer sounds. Finally, listen carefully to the sounds in your own body and stop noticing sounds around you.*

# SMELL

In some ways, smell is a very simple sense, compared to the others. There are only 5 million receptors and most people can detect only 10,000 odours. Every time we breathe in we bring microscopic bits of the outside world into contact with nerves in our noses. These nerves are unlike most others as they have one end dangling in the outside world and the other communicating with the brain. And this connection to the brain is itself rather special. Smell's first stop is the brain's emotion processing area, unlike sight and sound whose route is firstly through analytical areas. This is why smells are so good at evoking powerful memories and feelings.

## Activity

*Next time you are shopping, walk around a food market or the fresh food area of your usual supermarket. Identify three different smells, and notice what thoughts and feelings arise in connection with each.*

# TOUCH

Our skin measures about 2 square metres (21 square feet) and is the largest organ in our body. It has 200,000 receptors for cold, 500,000 for touch and 2,800,000 for pain, all unevenly distributed. The most sensitive parts of the skin can distinguish between two separate points (like pencil tips) applied only 3mm (⅛in) apart.

Like smell, touch is linked to our emotions and there is little processing at receptor level as the receptors are directly linked to the spinal cord and the brain.

## Activity

*Let yourself become aware of everything you are touching, either directly or indirectly – the texture of this book in your hand, the feel of your collar on your neck and your chair seat pressing up onto your thighs.*

# TASTE

This sense is in some ways our simplest; we certainly have fewer taste receptors, taste-buds, than any other type. They are renewed every ten days or so. We used to think there were only four separate tastes – sweet, sour, salty and bitter, but recent Japanese research has come up with 'umami' (which is related to glutamates) as a fifth and some scientists think there is a separate taste for fat. Taste is a survival tool – poisons are usually bitter, and unripe fruit is sour.

## Activity

*Next time you have a chance, try a food you haven't eaten before. Try to classify its taste by putting a little on the relevant parts of your tongue in turn: front – sweet, front sides – salty, back – bitter, far sides – sour.*

# SO HOW CLEVER ARE YOU?

*Many people have grown up with the self-belief that they either are intelligent or they're not. From an early age we will have overheard things like: 'Your Suzie's very bright, isn't she? I'll bet she's got a high IQ,' or, 'Little Jimmy's smart – he'll go far with that IQ.' Alternatively, of course, we may have been unfortunate enough to hear less favourable remarks.*

## BUT WHAT IS 'IQ'?

The whole idea of certain types of intelligence being a measure of someone's worth or potential became popular around the start of the twentieth century. William Stern and Alfred Binet designed tests to measure people's 'Intelligence Quotient' (IQ). These were based on language and numeracy. Entrance to schools and colleges was determined by how high a score you could get in an IQ test. Some, now thankfully discredited, researchers suggested that people with higher scores must, by definition, be superior to those with lower scores.

*Collins English Dictionary* defines intelligence as 'the capacity for understanding' – quite a broad definition. We now know that the narrow concept of intelligence as simply being skilled at mental arithmetic or using words is woefully limited. It is much more helpful to describe an 'intelligent' person as someone who can use their mind in a combination of ways.

## MULTIPLE INTELLIGENCES

In the last twenty years or so, psychologists have been suggesting that we have more than one 'intelligence', or capacity for understanding. Howard Gardner is one of the most notable, and his work in this area is constantly developing. Bill Lucas, of the Campaign for Learning, has helped to refine the idea of intelligences further, and Daniel Goleman made the concept of Emotional Intelligence particularly famous. Danah Zohar added Spiritual Intelligence to the debate. (See Resources, page 144.)

The table opposite shows common characteristics of each type of intelligence and activities for improving each one.

# THE 10 INTELLIGENCES

| INTELLIGENCE | CHARACTERISTICS | ACTIVITIES TO ENHANCE THIS INTELLIGENCE |
|---|---|---|
| 1 LINGUISTIC | A wide vocabulary and a good idea of correct spelling and grammar. Has often already read the book on which a film is based. Loves stories, languages and word play. | Choose a long word or a short phrase and see how many other words you can make with the letters. Have a go at some word puzzles and check the answers to understand how they work. |
| 2 MATHEMATICAL | Good at number puzzles and abstract problems. Understands statistics given out on the news and notices when they're misleading. Enjoys knowing how gadgets work and finding ways to fix them. Often makes numbered lists of tasks. | Look for occurrences of numbers in everyday life – keep a running total on your way to work: 'Number 14 bus, plus the 9.05 train (919), plus 13th-floor lift button (932)'. Find out how one of the mathematical concepts used in a newspaper (graphs or odds, for example) actually works. |
| 3 VISUAL | Good at diagrams and illustrations and aware of shape, colour and texture. Understands a new concept more quickly when it's supported by a picture or diagram. Probably doodles. | Try a non-verbal note-taking technique next time you're in a meeting. Imagine describing your job or a hobby to someone else without using words – what diagrams, maps, pictures would you use? |
| 4 PHYSICAL | Enjoys physical activity and is (or once was) possibly good at sport or dancing. Is good with his or her hands and may use hand gestures when speaking. Is often keen to take part in team-building activities or group exercises. | At least once a day, move away from your work area and do something physical and become aware of other muscles than the ones you usually use. This doesn't have to be noticeable or embarrassing; for example, you could stretch up to the highest shelf in your office, or take your next phone call standing up. |
| 5 MUSICAL | Good at recognizing different rhythms and types of music and able to remember melodies. May be, or have been, involved in making music. His or her mood is likely to be affected by music. | Next time you listen to some music, either on purpose or by accident, try to pick out the different instruments. When you hear an unfamiliar melody (even someone else's mobile ring tone), play it back in your mind three times. |
| 6 SOCIAL | Enjoys being with other people, in both formal and informal settings. Good at noticing other people's moods and listening to others, so is likely to be sought out for advice. | Find opportunities to talk and listen to someone you haven't talked with before – even just a few words at the coffee machine. Volunteer for an activity that involves talking to everyone, such as organizing a leaving card collection. |
| 7 ENVIRONMENTAL | Good understanding of the natural world – plants, animals, geography and the climate – and interested in the environment. May look after pets or other animals. | Next time you walk somewhere, make a point of noticing natural things. For example, look at the shapes of clouds, the direction of the breeze, any greenery, animals and birds. Look up anything you didn't recognize later. |
| 8 PRACTICAL | Good at sorting things out and putting things together. Interested in how theories work in practice and so likely to come up with workable solutions to problems. | Next time you need a small practical task doing, note down what stages you think you'd need to go through to do it yourself. Then when the person arrives to do it, compare what he or she actually does with your notes. |
| 9 EMOTIONAL | Aware of their own feelings and moods, and how experiences affect them. May set personal goals and keep a diary or journal. Interested in self-development and may have sought counselling for self-improvement. | Once a week, spend time on your own and think about a recent event, such as a meeting, and write down what happened, who was involved and what was said. Then write how you felt at each stage. Look closely at a picture and identify the feelings it arouses in you. |
| 10 SPIRITUAL | Aware of the values and principles that lie behind actions and concerned with fundamental questions about life. He or she may be, or have been, involved in community service and is likely to hold well-developed beliefs, although not necessarily any particular religious faith. | Look for interviews in the media in which people talk about their values and beliefs. Notice their arguments and reasons for their views, and look for words which describe values and principles. This will help you to became more exposed to the language of spiritual intelligence. Can you apply any of the words to your own ideas and beliefs? |

# THE GENDER GAP?

It is obvious that there are many physical differences between men and women – why should that be any different for our brains? The problem comes when someone suggests that such differences make one gender superior to the other.

We now know that while the male human brain weighs on average about ten per cent more than the female brain, certain areas in women's brains contain more nerve cells than men's. And we also know that, for as long as intelligence tests have been in use, women and men have consistently scored equally well.

Brain size and cell count don't really help us, therefore, to understand male and female thinking, because we still don't really understand how structural differences influence brain function. It's probable that male and female brains work at the same capacity, but process information differently.

Using brain imaging equipment, scientists have observed that men and women complete the same tasks in similar times, with similar results, but that different parts of the brain are used. Other research shows that there are tasks which members of one sex perform more successfully than those of the other. For example, women can often recall sections of a text or lists of objects better than men, whereas men will perform better in tests which ask them to rotate an image mentally to solve a problem, such as finding their way around a town centre. This doesn't mean that men get lost less often than women. It just means they find their way around differently – the men by imagining the streets from different directions, and the women by recalling landmarks on the journey.

## ACTIVITY

Think of a woman and a man that you know in your work environment. Notice how each of them operates in certain situations, and then think about how you work in the same circumstances. You are not making judgments now about which method is best, simply observing any differences and similarities. Of course, this won't tell you how all men and women would think in similar situations, but it will help you become more aware of different thinking styles. For example:

| | JANE | JOHN | ME |
|---|---|---|---|
| **Making decision about who to ask onto committee** | Listened a lot, then asked lots of questions, but made few notes. | Had his own idea of preferred choice, but asked us all to speak in turn with our views. | Listed criteria, then made up my mind very quickly. |

# OUR BRAINS AND AGEING

Most of us have probably grown up with the notion that the brain starts its dying process almost as soon as we're born. It is true that many areas of our brains do not regenerate naturally, but, as we have already seen, much of the brain's function relies on the millions of interconnections between brain cells, not on how many of them we've got. It also looks as though the fact that older people's brains weigh less is more to do with dehydration than brain capability.

Scientists are now questioning earlier research that 'proved' that older people were less intelligent than younger ones. Most of the tests simply gave groups of people the same time-limited IQ test. Older people got lower scores so testers drew a simple conclusion – young people are cleverer than old people. Once testing became more sophisticated and such factors as someone's familiarity with IQ tests and their understanding of the language used, were taken into account, older people did equally well. In their book, *The Age Heresy*, Tony Buzan and Raymond Keene refer to current research that is changing the way we think about ageing and intelligence.

Unfortunately, the myth about loss of brain power as we grow older persists, both in Western culture generally and in the workplace in particular. Of course, many degenerative illnesses do strike older people disproportionately, so most of us will be able to think of someone who has become confused or less able to think clearly than they once were. But it isn't an inevitable consequence of ageing – you will be able to think of many people, either famous or who you know personally, who seem to be getting better with age.

The good news is that by getting into the habit of doing things that stimulate your vital brain connections, you'll be keeping your brain fit as it gets older.

## ACTIVITY: 'DO SOMETHING DIFFERENT TODAY'

Write this phrase boldly in whatever way suits your diary. For example, use a mini sticky note in a paper diary, or a flag in your electronic organizer. Keep moving the flag through the diary so that doing something differently becomes a daily habit.
It doesn't have to be anything that takes a lot of extra time. You could:
• Use a different route to the photocopier.
• Choose a different magazine to read on your journey to work.
• Try a different sandwich filling.
Then spend a few minutes thinking about what that new experience has taught you.

# LIMBER UP
## Some mental dexterity exercises

(The answers are on page 139.)

## A PIECE OF CAKE

What is the lowest number of straight cuts you need to make to divide this cake into eight equal pieces?

## ALL IN THE FAMILY

At a wedding there were six people called Chris and this is how they were related to each other. Chris is Chris's cousin, Chris is Chris's husband's sister and Chris is married to Chris.

What is the highest number of women that could be present?

## COUNT ON IT

The numbers in each triangle have the same relationship. Fill in the missing number.

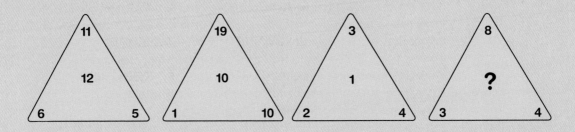

# LOST LETTERS

Fill each bracket with a letter that fits on the end of the word on the left and fits at the start of the word on the right.

HEART( )EATER
PLANE( )AUGHT
SUPER( )LIGHT
LARGE( )OTTER

# COUNTRY CODE

In this code, each country has a value. What is the value of Turkey?

# LUCKY 13

Find another way to make 13 using the letters below.

ELEVEN
+
TWO

# FOLLOW ON

What are the next two numbers in the sequence:

2, 11, 6, 19, 10, 27, 14, 35, ?, ?

# ODD ONE OUT

Can you find the odd one out?

1 UUSTGA

2 AAYJURN

3 CHARM

4 DUSYTEA

5 LUYJ

6 PREESTMEB

# 2 TYPES OF THINKING

*Like nearly everything else in this book, thinking can be thought about in lots of ways. Down the centuries great thinkers have applied their minds to finding out what goes on when we think.*

## WAYS OF THINKING

Every day we apply our brains to questions and problems and there are many possible approaches to finding **solutions**. In fact, we often use more than one way of thinking at the same time:

- turning an idea over in your mind
- examining all sides of an argument
- reflecting on something that's happened
- looking for connections
- breaking a process into parts
- imagining what might happen in the future
- remembering something from the past
- being aware of what is happening around you

... and no doubt you can think of other methods we use in our daily thinking schedule.

## *A different approach may provide the answer*

When we are trying to find ways to keep our brains fit to deal with all the things we have to cope with in our working day, it probably helps to simplify things a bit. Basically, there are two types of thinking which we could apply to the items in the list above: **analytical** and **creative**.

# ANALYTICAL AND CREATIVE THINKING

|  | ANALYTICAL | CREATIVE |
|---|---|---|
| Mostly uses | logic, facts, figures, data | imagination, intuition |
| Approach | narrows things down, time-limited | widens things out, not time-limited |
| Method | vertical (deep, narrow, probing), linear | lateral (all ideas ok even those not thought to be linked) |
| Uses | building a case, drawing conclusions from data | breaking a stalemate, changing perceptions, challenging assumptions |
| Most active brain hemisphere | left | right |

## ACTIVITY

Choose a decision you will soon have to make. It can be big (shall I move house?, for example) or small (shall I have coffee or tea?).

Now think about the decision in the two different ways:

| ANALYTICALLY | CREATIVELY |
|---|---|
| What is the current situation?<br>What do I want?<br>What are my criteria?<br>What information do I have?<br>What information do I need?<br>What are my choices?<br>Which choices match my criteria?<br>WOho will be able to help me implement the choice? | Imagine a time in the future when the decision has been made.<br>Draw a picture of yourself successfully doing/using the solution.<br>What feels like the best solution? |

We'll look in detail at analytical and creative techniques later on. For now, just notice how different each way of thinking felt and make a note of any insights you actually got about the decision you were considering. It may have been only an exercise, but most people report that having the chance to focus on an issue does bring some new thoughts to the surface.

# HOW WE ORGANIZE
# OUR THINKING

## *Don't eat the tablecloth*

We all have ways of organizing our knowledge and experience, although we may not be conscious of them. If we didn't have our personal theories, frameworks, maps and concepts we would become ill trying to make sense of all the experiences we are bombarded with every day. Our ability to recognize and make judgments about things and then put them away in mental boxes helps us to cope with the world. For example, if we have a box in our mind marked 'food' we know what to do with the items on our plate at dinner time, and we don't attempt to eat the tablecloth. We don't have to test every item around us to see what is edible.

Of course, this very ability to **identify** and **compartmentalize** is one of the things that can block our best thinking. We may use very simplistic labelling (for example, tastes good/tastes bad). The labels may have come about through limited experience and so may stop us thinking clearly about what is happening now.

## PREVIOUS EXPERIENCES

An individual's ability to use his or her thinking processes will partly depend on previous learning experiences. Remember how hard it was as a child to make up your mind about which sweets to choose in the sweetshop, especially if you were told to 'Hurry up'. Then, when you'd made a choice, you were asked 'What did you choose that for? You'll make a mess.' In such simple, and often kindly meant ways, we've all been discouraged from using our thinking processes and become distrustful of our ability to do so. We worry about taking too long and making wrong choices.

## *Anyone can think creatively*

Our workplaces don't always help. Traditionally, analytical thinking has been valued more highly than creative thinking and many people have got out of the habit of even trying to think creatively.

# QUESTIONNAIRE

Try this questionnaire to see where your true abilities lie. Read each pair of statements and mark which you prefer – they are not exact opposites. Sometimes the choice will be obvious to you, but in other cases, you may want to mark both statements. Please choose one, even if it is only a very slight preference. Answer according to what you really think and feel, not how you think you ought to respond.

**A** I spend some of every day 'pottering about'
**B** I hate wasting time

**A** When I have a decision to make, the first thing I do is make a drink
**B** When I have a decision to make, the first thing I do is to gather all the information I'll need

**A** I enjoy daydreaming
**B** I dislike daydreaming

**A** I revel in being a bit different
**B** I like to fit in with the crowd

**A** People might describe me as talkative
**B** People might describe me as thoughtful

**A** I read around a subject to find out what others think before I commit myself
**B** I make my mind up before finding out others' opinions

**A** I like using unusual words
**B** I like using precise words

**A** I prefer puzzles that could have lots of answers
**B** I don't really like doing puzzles

**A** I'm sensitive to the working environment – I can't think properly if my surroundings are unpleasant
**B** Once I'm concentrating on the job in hand I hardly notice my surroundings

**A** I would like to be thought of as imaginative
**B** I would like to be thought of as logical

**A** I like to bounce ideas around with other people
**B** I like to work out my own strategies before other people contribute

**A** I believe intuition has a place in decision-making
**B** I do not believe intuition has a place in decision-making

**A** I feel stressed if I'm asked to come up with a structured approach to a problem
**B** I feel stressed if I'm not given clear guidelines within which to work

**A** I like to hear what famous people think about current issues
**B** I'm not interested in what famous people think about current issues

**A** 'Big picture' questions are best for starting discussions
**B** Probing questions are best for getting to the facts

**A** I like to be allowed to voice my opinions, even if they may be unpopular
**B** If I know my opinion might be unpopular I'll keep it to myself

**A** I like abstract ideas
**B** I like practical ideas

**A** I was not always happy at school, especially when I felt the rules were constricting
**B** I found school rules helpful – they provide structure

**A** I like taking things apart to see how they work
**B** I like putting things together to make them work

**A** I like group creativity sessions
**B** I like thinking things through on my own

**A** I believe mistakes can be useful if they lead to fresh ideas
**B** I believe mistakes can be useful if they lead to getting things right

# SCORING

Now tot up your scores to see where your true abilities lie.

**Mostly As**

**STRENGTHS** You have high creativity and will probably be able to generate ideas easily and work with hunches. You are comfortable with the ambiguous and get frustrated if you feel constrained. You do not mind being thought of as a bit unorthodox.

**AREAS TO WORK ON** You need to make sure you don't miss detail, particularly if you're on your own.

**Equal numbers of As and Bs**

**STRENGTHS** You have a pretty balanced approach to thinking. You are equally happy working in a group or on your own, and you will probably feel comfortable using a range of thinking techniques.

**AREAS TO WORK ON** You need to make sure that you don't let the fear of taking a risk hold back your creativity.

**Mostly Bs**

**STRENGTHS** You have well-developed analytical skills and can understand complex sets of data. You like issues to be well defined and you get frustrated with vagueness. You are good at being methodical.

**AREAS TO WORK ON** You need to ensure that you listen well to others' ideas – they may reach the same decisions as you by different routes.

# There is no right or wrong way of thinking

This questionnaire is not designed to be judgmental. There is no 'best' way to be. The important thing is to identify where your thinking skills may be lacking and to look for opportunities to try out thinking methods that you are unfamiliar with. You may have surprised yourself with your answers and come out with more As than you would have expected – in most sectors, even if we might like to be a bit unorthodox, it feels safer to conform. Current research is consistently demonstrating that organizations that encourage their staff to use their creativity are more likely to succeed.

# LEARNING

The concept of **learning**, as opposed to **teaching**, has rightly become very popular in recent years. You may be familiar with the old saying: 'You can lead a horse to water but you cannot make it drink.' This describes how many people first experienced being taught. They were put into a classroom, and someone talked to them, probably at some length, about a subject. Whether the student learned anything in this scenario was a matter of chance. Perhaps enough facts would sink in to get through an examination, especially if there was some threat or promise attached. But generally, such methods of teaching have been shown to be largely a waste of time.

In fact, of course, we always do learn something from each experience. In the situation just described, it may be: 'Well, I've learned not to go to that class again without a novel to read behind my textbook.'

## LEARNING FROM EXPERIENCE

When we learned to walk as children, we didn't find it necessary to go on a course, watch an instructional video or look on the web. No one sat us down and explained physiology to us. We just kept on having a go, falling over, finding things to hold on to and having another go. And we still learn like that as adults, however sophisticated we think we are.

Much of the time, we do not even realize that we *are* learning. We don't tend to use the language of learning in our everyday lives, but instead say things like:

*'I'd like to have a go at that'*

*'I wonder why that happened'*

*'Oh, I see why that went wrong'*

*'Next time, I'll try it another way'*

# LEARNING STYLES

Peter Honey and Alan Mumford have researched learning in many organizations over many years. They identified what they called an 'experiential learning cycle', and discovered that there are four 'learning styles', which can be plotted on to the cycle as shown.

Most people will have a preference for one or other of these learning styles, although this does not mean they do not use the others. The trick is to get better at the others in order to learn throughout all the experiences that we have.

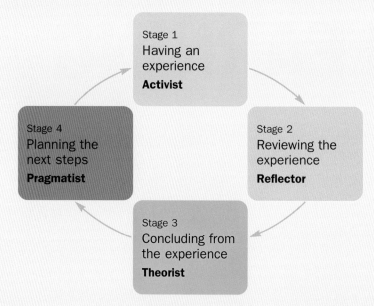

**Stage 1**
Having an experience
**Activist**

**Stage 2**
Reviewing the experience
**Reflector**

**Stage 3**
Concluding from the experience
**Theorist**

**Stage 4**
Planning the next steps
**Pragmatist**

## Activist style

- enjoy new experiences, and being 'thrown in at the deep end'
- like the excitement of a drama or crisis
- respond well to ideas outside policy constraints
- need to bounce ideas off other people
- won't appreciate being told to read the manual before plugging in their new PC

## Theorist style

- work well with theories and concepts
- enjoy being stretched intellectually
- respond well in structured situations
- don't appreciate doing things which don't have an apparent purpose
- don't like things which seem to them shallow or 'gimmicky'

## Reflector style

- are good at painstaking research
- like having the chance to sit back and think
- appreciate having time to think before acting
- don't like being pushed into doing something without time to prepare
- are worried by crises and time pressure

## Pragmatist style

- are good at seeing links between concepts and their everyday use
- work well on practical activities like action plans
- respond well to the chance to put things into practice immediately
- need guidelines and instructions before having a go
- don't appreciate learning that's not immediately useful

Honey and Mumford have designed a questionnaire which enables you to get an accurate picture of your own learning style. See page 144 for details of where to get this questionnaire.

# ACTIVITY

Think back over the last week. Identify something that you have done which you would like to think of again as a 'learning experience'. It doesn't have to be a major event, like learning a new software package. It could be something like talking to a colleague about a project you're both involved in. Then take it round the learning cycle. Make notes about each stage. For example:

## 1 Having the experience

Last Tuesday I spent an hour with Sue, talking about improving the post recording system. We'd both brought examples of ways we'd seen it done in our previous companies. We'd previously agreed to take the best bits from each system. We started the meeting off OK but ended up having a bit of an argument, and not agreeing on a new system.

## 2 Reviewing the experience

I listened well at first to what Sue had to say about her system. I got a bit irritated with her when she kept straying off the point and reminiscing about her old company. I think I'd done a bit more research than she had. I felt rather pressured for time because I had to get away early on Tuesday to pick my daughter up from nursery.

## 3 Concluding from the experience

I think we got into the argument because I wasn't very clear about why I was irritated. I also think I went into the meeting having made my mind up that 'my' system was the best.

## 4 Planning the next steps

In a similar situation I'd be much clearer about my time pressures and more assertive if the other person goes off the point. With Sue, I need to explain why I felt frustrated. I need to make sure I have the opportunity to go through my system too.

Of course, no one has enough time to go through this process this methodically after every experience. But if you get into the habit of doing it once in a while, and certainly more often mentally, you'll soon be far more of an all-round learner.

# PERSONALITY TYPE
# AND THINKING

*You may have done various personality tests during your life. Sometimes you see the result and think, 'Yes, that's me, all right. It's uncanny.' At other times your reaction may be much more sceptical. In fact it may actually be an aspect of your personality that's affecting your response to the test.*

One of the most important things to remember whenever we think about personality types is that there is no 'best'. However, understanding ourselves and others in terms of personality types can help to explain why we get all our best ideas when we're working with some people and simply get frustrated when trying to work with others.

The Swiss psychiatrist Carl Jung was the first to investigate how our personalities affect how we deal with information. He discovered that people fall into different groups depending on how they prefer to handle information (**S**ensors or i**N**tuitors) and make decisions (**T**hinkers and **F**eelers). As a shorthand these are referred to as S, N, T, F. The initial N was chosen for the iNtuitors to avoid confusion with another aspect of Jung's work – the difference between Extroverts and Introverts.

## WHAT DOES IT ALL MEAN?

Sensing and iNtuiting are about how we prefer to take in and process information. Sensing people will be likely to use their senses, whilst iNtuiting individuals are more likely to use insights, associations and connections. Neither is better than the other, and each can use the other's style – just not quite so comfortably. If you are an S working with an N you can complement each other very well. New ideas would be no good without the practical information needed to put them into practice. High quality production needs forward-looking products to capture new markets.

Thinking and Feeling are about how we prefer to make decisions. Ts are not 'unfeeling' and Fs are perfectly able to think. This is simply about which you're likely to use first. Both are rational, it's just that Ts and Fs have different ideas about what 'rational' means. Once again, neither is better than the other.

# ACTIVITY

Which responses most closely match what you'd be thinking in the given situations? Choose an S or an N, and a T or an F each time.

**1 A colleague brings her answerphone to you in pieces, after trying to fix it.**

**S:** 'I know how these work. Hand it over and I'll put it back together for you.'

*or*

**N:** 'Have you checked in the manual? Have you rung the manufacturer? Has it happened before?'

*and*

**T:** 'Here's my manual, you can borrow it. You could try fixing it, or you could find out which would be cheaper, repair or replacement.'

*or*

**F:** 'Oh, poor you. Do you think you've missed many calls while it's been out of action? You can borrow mine if you need to.'

**2 Your boss suggests a change to one of your procedures.**

**S:** 'I can see how that would work.'

*or*

**N:** 'It's a bit like the way we used to do it in my previous company.'

*and*

**T:** 'It will work if we get the right software.'

*or*

**F:** 'I hope she's taken everyone's views into account.'

**3 Your colleague asks how many people you think will come to the Friday lunchtime seminar you're organizing.**

**S:** 'I'll have to check with all the other sections to get their attendance lists.'

*or*

**N:** 'Oh, about 40.'

*and*

**T:** '37.'

*or*

**F:** 'It probably depends on what else is going on that day and how tired people are at the end of the week.'

**4 A bit of an argument is developing at the weekly meeting.**

**S:** thinks: 'Why can't they keep to the point?'

*or*

**N:** switches off and gets on with a things to do list.

*and*

**T** thinks: 'They're not being very businesslike.'

*or*

**F** thinks: 'How can I calm things down?'

# 3 PACKING YOUR MENTAL BRIEFCASE

*'Pen, organizer, mobile phone, meeting agenda, magazine, apple, ideas, insights, reflections ...'*

Do you ever give any thought to what mental skills you'll need for the day ahead? Most of us are quite used to the idea of making sure we've read the documents for the first meeting of the day, but we probably won't have thought, 'Oh, I'd better make sure my logical thinking is ready.'

## *Is your mind ready for the demands of the day ahead?*

In the past, when someone started a new job, they'd get a job description (if they were lucky) and were just told to get on with it. Maybe this is a bit of an over-simplification, but many people over 45 would say that sounds like their experience.

Today, you are much more likely to have guidelines about *how* you're expected to work as well as what you're expected to do. Often, these expectations are set out in the form of **'competences'**. Competences are statements about the abilities you're expected to demonstrate right across your job.

Have a look at the list of competences opposite. It may appear rather daunting at first, but if you look at it in terms of a typical day, you'll see that you're probably already coming up to expectations.

# COMPETENCES

| | |
|---|---|
| **Initiative** | Act on own initiative. Understand when action is needed. |
| **Creativity** | Challenge preconceived ideas. Find innovative approaches to problems. |
| **Resilience** | Maintain performance under pressure.<br>Respond flexibly to short- and long-term changes in priorities. |
| **Expertise and specialist skills** | Continuously develop knowledge and skills relevant to this job, and consider development to the next career move. |
| **Analysis and judgment** | Recognize importance of information in relation to current issues.<br>Evaluate and reach decisions and workable solutions. |
| **Service delivery** | Meet needs of internal and external customers. Seek out and offer new approaches. |
| **Dealing with people** | Act in a way that shows respect for others. Awareness of impact of own behaviour on others. Provide direction and management to others as appropriate.<br>Work co-operatively and supportively with colleagues. |
| **Communication** | Express ideas and convey information clearly and confidently. |

# COMPETENCE DIARY

Have a look at your work diary for tomorrow. Think about which competence you'll be using as you do each activity.

| TIME | ACTIVITY | COMPETENCE |
|---|---|---|
| **08.30** | Arrive | |
| **08.35** | Coffee at desk. Read papers for meeting | Expertise and specialist skills |
| **08.45** | Meeting with Mike to decide budget strategy | Dealing with others, expertise, creativity |
| **11.30** | Brief June about budget | Communication |

# WHAT YOU BRING WITH YOU TO THIS JOB

When we first looked for work, we were encouraged to include details of our outside interests on our job applications to give prospective employers an idea of what sort of people we were. Now, it is much more useful to describe outside activities in terms that employers will recognize as being useful in the workplace.

## MAKING THE MOST OF YOUR ASSETS

Emphasizing skills used outside the office that employers will find useful is particularly important for women who are returning to work after some years spent bringing up a family. For example, getting two children to and from school and activities becomes 'Organize and operate transport schedules'. This is not 'spin' because she would use the example of the school run in the interview. First, write as comprehensive a list as you can of all the things you do in your life. Think of things under the headings of: Home, School, Hobbies, Jobs, Community, Spiritual and any more you can think of:

**HOME**
Organize family's diary
Plan and shop for meals
Cook
Resolve conflicts

**PREVIOUS JOBS**
Waitress in college bar
Checkout operator at
    supermarket
Book-keeper

**SCHOOL**
Form prefect
Ran chess club
Organized sixth form fashion
    show
Took part in debating
    competition
Played recorder

**HOBBIES**
Reading fiction and
    biographies
Swimming
Going out with friends
Pottery class

**COMMUNITY**
Take the minutes of Parent
    Teachers Association
    committee
On rota to help at Cub Scouts
Used to volunteer at
    Samaritans

**SPIRITUAL**
Sing in gospel choir

Then, try to identify what thinking skills and competences you use in each, and add them to your list on the previous page.

Now imagine you are presenting your brain portfolio to a prospective employer. How are you going to sell yourself?

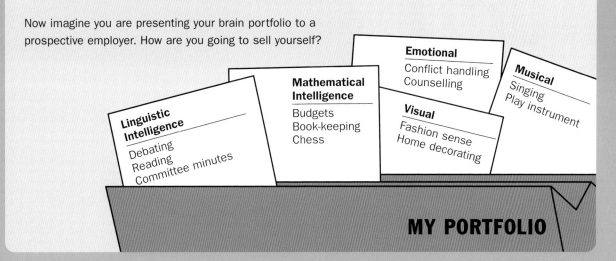

**Emotional**
Conflict handling
Counselling

**Musical**
Singing
Play instrument

**Mathematical Intelligence**
Budgets
Book-keeping
Chess

**Visual**
Fashion sense
Home decorating

**Linguistic Intelligence**
Debating
Reading
Committee minutes

**MY PORTFOLIO**

# CASE STUDY

Suresh had worked for some years as a warehouse manager for a medium-sized distribution company. He felt that he was good at his job, and enjoyed it most of the time. He liked the occasional pressure of rush orders and the need to motivate the team of packers and handlers. He was also good at sorting out minor rows and disputes and had a reputation as a fair man to work for.

He was, however, beginning to wonder whether he would progress further. He'd always fancied the idea of being a salesman – more at the front line and less tied down to the clocking-on system.

One Friday, the company newsletter arrived on Suresh's desk and seemed to fall open at the 'Company Opportunities' page. The sales team was looking for a Junior Sales Rep. Suresh closed the page with a sigh. 'They'd never even consider me,' he thought.

That evening, he had to be at his son's school at 7pm to chair the working party the school governors had set up to look at the feasibility of the school buying a mini-bus.

On Saturday morning, Suresh dropped his son at football, then went to visit the Chairman of the Chamber of Commerce. Suresh's community newspaper needed advertisers and he wanted to convince the Chairman that local businesses would get customers through the paper.

Over Sunday lunch, Suresh told his wife about the ad for the sales team and how he'd love to go for it but his experience would be too limited. She smiled and ticked off on her fingers all the areas of his life which Suresh could use to convince the Sales Manager he'd be good on the team.

'Initiative – great idea to approach the Chamber of Commerce. Selling abilities – look how you convinced the local authority to put up half the funds for the mini-bus. Teamwork – all the committees you're on. Dealing with people – remember how you sorted out that row between John and Jeff at work?'

So Suresh spent the rest of Sunday updating his CV, writing his portfolio and filling in the application form.

Next Friday, he got the job.

# PERSONAL COMPETENCE
# AUDIT

This questionnaire will help to highlight where you're already demonstrating the competences and where you might need to develop. It may give you some insights or it might confirm what you already knew – or guessed.

It contains 40 statements. Think about yourself as widely as you like, both at work and outside the workplace, and circle A, B, C or D alongside each number in the scoring table opposite.

**A**  **Circle A** if you think the statement is always or nearly always true of you; if you strongly agree; if you always or nearly always behave or feel the way indicated by the statement.

**B**  **Circle B** if you think the statement is generally true of you; if you fairly definitely agree; if you quite often behave or feel the way indicated by the statement.

**C**  **Circle C** if you think the statement is occasionally true of you; if you partly agree; if you occasionally behave or feel the way indicated by the statement.

**D**  **Circle D** if you think the statement is definitely not true of you; if you disagree; if you hardly ever or never behave or feel the way indicated by the statement.

1  I am prepared to tackle tasks that other people ignore.
2  I use creative ways of looking at problems.
3  I admit to my mistakes and take action to prevent or minimize any problems caused by them.
4  I regularly attend seminars about subjects to do with my work.
5  I can quickly get to grips with large volumes of information.
6  I make sure that things I say will get done do get done.
7  People would describe me as fair and reasonable.
8  When I give other people verbal information they say I am clear and concise.
9  I know how and where to get the resources I need to do my job.
10  I am interested in new approaches to tasks and I welcome ideas from other people.
11  People would describe me as someone who can 'think on their feet'.
12  I could describe my company's business and how it works to a newcomer.
13  If I'm involved in a project I am aware of the stage we're at and how well it's going.

14 My customers, both inside and outside the organization, know what I can and cannot do for them.

15 When I'm working in a team I take part in developing that team's goals and plans.

16 I do not have difficulty getting other people to understand my point of view.

17 When necessary, I take the initiative without waiting for direction from those above me.

18 I offer a range of solutions when I can.

19 I have a reputation as someone who delivers on time.

20 I belong to the business and specialist associations relevant to my work, and go to their meetings whenever I can.

21 When I have to make a presentation or write a report I spend time researching and preparing.

22 I work with my customers to help to identify and resolve problems.

23 When I'm working with other people I like to make sure we all know what to expect from each other.

24 I recognize and avoid jargon and clichés in my speaking and writing.

25 If a situation has reached a stalemate, I take action to move it on.

26 I think all ideas are worth looking at, whoever suggests them.

27 I work effectively in stressful situations.

28 I am well-informed about what's going on in the world that might be relevant to my job.

29 I can identify which organizational objectives relate to my work.

30 I try to look for reasons to do something rather than reasons not to.

31 I am aware of the impact on other people of my behaviour and actions.

32 I speak at meetings on behalf of my team or organization.

33 I look for opportunities to take on responsibilities in new areas.

34 I often introduce new ideas at work.

35 When I'm under pressure, I still keep long-term priorities in mind.

36 I give consistent advice.

37 I base decisions on practical experience.

38 I identify the benefits in a situation for others as well as myself, aiming for a win-win outcome.

39 I prefer to get disagreements out into the open, rather than have an uncomfortable atmosphere.

40 Colleagues often ask me to comment on their letters, reports and so on before they send them.

## SCORING TABLE

| 17 A | 18 A | 19 A | 20 A | 21 A | 22 A | 23 A | 24 A |
|---|---|---|---|---|---|---|---|
| B | B | B | B | B | B | B | B |
| C | C | C | C | C | C | C | C |
| D | D | D | D | D | D | D | D |

| 1 A | 2 A | 3 A | 4 A | 5 A | 6 A | 7 A | 8 A |
|---|---|---|---|---|---|---|---|
| B | B | B | B | B | B | B | B |
| C | C | C | C | C | C | C | C |
| D | D | D | D | D | D | D | D |

| 25 A | 26 A | 27 A | 28 A | 29 A | 30 A | 31 A | 32 A |
|---|---|---|---|---|---|---|---|
| B | B | B | B | B | B | B | B |
| C | C | C | C | C | C | C | C |
| D | D | D | D | D | D | D | D |

| 9 A | 10 A | 11 A | 12 A | 13 A | 14 A | 15 A | 16 A |
|---|---|---|---|---|---|---|---|
| B | B | B | B | B | B | B | B |
| C | C | C | C | C | C | C | C |
| D | D | D | D | D | D | D | D |

| 33 A | 34 A | 35 A | 36 A | 37 A | 38 A | 39 A | 40 A |
|---|---|---|---|---|---|---|---|
| B | B | B | B | B | B | B | B |
| C | C | C | C | C | C | C | C |
| D | D | D | D | D | D | D | D |

# SCORING

To calculate your score give yourself 4 points for every A, 3 points for every B, 2 points for every C and 1 point for every D. Then add up the total number of points in each column. The eight columns correspond to the eight competences on page 35.

# INTERPRETING YOUR RESULT

The questionnaire is designed so that the highest scores indicate competences in which you are already strong. The maximum score for any competence is 20 and the lowest possible is 5. Lower scores show where you may need to do some development.

Look over your scores. Are there any that stand out as definitely low? Or are they all about the same? If two or three are definitely lower, then it would be a good idea to make these your priority development areas. If they are all about the same, choose the two or three competences that seem most relevant to your current – or future – job.

Of course, this questionnaire is wholly subjective, and you need to remember that you are probably being harder on yourself than anyone else would be.

It's important to remember that development includes continuing with the things you're already doing well. As we've seen, we learn from experience, so identifying our existing skills so that we can transfer them to our weaker areas is also a vital activity.

# COMPETENCE REVIEW AND ACTION PLAN

List the three competences that you are going to work on.

Now write a list of how each competence applies in your job.

Then write three things that you are going to do to develop each one. This may not be an easy task. After all, it's probably because you don't always know what to do in a particular competence area that's led to a low score in the first place. So you could use the questions that you answered with C or D as prompts for ideas if you are stuck.

# THE COMPETENCE
# LADDER

Think about something you currently do almost without thinking, such as driving a car. Even if you don't drive, you may find it a helpful analogy.

Before you even wanted to learn to drive, you saw cars moving along the streets. You had no idea what was involved in driving. Then came the day of your first lesson. All of a sudden, there's a huge amount to take in, about the car, other drivers, the road, the pedestrians. Somehow, you make it from A to B, but you aren't really driving yet – you're all too aware of all there is still to learn.

Soon, though, you're ready to take your test. You can do it, but you're going to have to concentrate like mad. You think through every manoeuvre, making sure you do everything in the right order.

**UNCONSCIOUS COMPETENCE**
*I'm doing it without thinkng*

**NEW SKILLS WALL**

**CONSCIOUS INCOMPETENCE**
*I know what a lot I've got to learn*

**CONSCIOUS COMPETENCE**
*I can do it but need to think about it*

**UNCONSCIOUS INCOMPETENCE**
*I don't even know what there is to learn*

Once you've passed, you can go out on the road on your own, and before too long you're able to drive while listening to the radio, talking to your passengers or enjoying the scenery – hardly thinking about the driving at all.

You've climbed the 'competence ladder' and when you reach the top you may see other ladders stretching away into the distance.

# MAKING THE MOST OF YOUR
# JOURNEY TO WORK

It may be that you need your journey time to recharge your physical batteries. A little nap on the train can be very refreshing. Your favourite music in the car or your personal stereo may help you to relax.

But sometimes, a journey is just dead time. This is a waste if you want to arrive at work with your brain fired up and ready to go.

## ACTIVITIES TO WARM UP YOUR THINKING

**1** Imagine that you have the task of compiling the test questions for a quiz programme, using your own job as the competitor's chosen topic.

**2** Focus on an impending task. Fill in this box:

| Facts you know and can use | Areas of ignorance you can do something about |
|---|---|
| **A** | **B** |
| **C** | **D** |
| Facts you know and could use more or better | Areas of ignorance you need to discover |

How will you convert: Cs into As?  Ds into Bs?  Bs into As?

# *Warm up your mental muscles on the way to work and arrive alert and prepared ...*

**3** Think about what you did yesterday evening, even if it was simply watching TV. Take it round the **learning cycle** (see page 30–31). Identify at least one thing you could say you've learned from it.

**4** Imagine a situation you're facing today. Put yourself into the picture.

**What will you see as you look around?**
**What will you hear? Touch? Smell? Taste?**

Now imagine one of the other people who'll be involved.
**What will they see and hear as they look at you?**

**5** Choose a famous person from the current news, or that you can see pictured in someone's newspaper. Call to mind a problem you are facing. How would that famous person solve it?

# 4 GETTING DOWN TO WORK

## DISTRACTIONS

'I just get started and the phone rings.'
'Have you got a minute?'
'I know I had that file here somewhere.'
'I'll just finish my coffee, then I'll think about tomorrow's meeting.'
'I need to sort out these files before I can settle down to that report.'
'Mmmm, that was a great weekend ...'

Recognize any of these?

There are all sorts of distractions that can stop us working and thinking. Some of them are external – other people, and the environment in which we are working, distract us – and others are internal – we do them to ourselves. Even some of the external distractions are more about how we handle them than what other people do to us.

## FIVE WAYS TO RECLAIM YOUR SPACE

1 Make sure your work space *is* a space – not just the top of a pile. Clear away all the stuff not related to the thing you're working on.
2 If you haven't read those torn-out newspaper or magazine articles in the three months since you saved them – you never will. Throw them away.
3 Aim for a full wastepaper basket and an empty desk every day.
4 Use a pad or notebook to record calls and messages – scraps of paper and sticky notes get buried. Keep the pad to hand so you can make a note if you're interrupted and can quickly get back to what you were doing.
5 Make sure your phone is on the side you don't write with – then you won't have to reach across and mess up your space every time you make a note while you're talking.

Whether you work at home or in an office, open plan or private space, behind a reception desk or a shop counter, you can have *some* control over your environment. Arrange your work space so that when you come to start some brain work you can get right to it.

# FILING

The invention of the filing cabinet was a revolution in office life and meant we could now keep everything. And with the arrival of carbon paper and later the photocopier, we could keep duplicate copies of everything. We have got so entrenched in this habit that many people print off emails and keep those too.

Research has shown that people ignore about 85 per cent of the paper they keep and that 45 per cent of it is also kept somewhere else by someone else. Many of us are afraid to throw anything away in case we need it the very next day, and perhaps you can think of one time when that very thing happened. But what about all the dozens of times it didn't happen – you threw a piece of paper away and the world didn't stop.

Put a note in your diary every week to spend 30 minutes going through the papers you have accumulated and work out which fall into the 'I'll never need this again' category or the 'Someone else has got this' category.

Work out a filing system that works for you – it doesn't have to be clever or elaborate. However, don't wait for the right time or the perfect system before you get organized – get on with it now.

## CASE STUDY

Jane decided to fulfill her dream and leave her organization to set up as a freelance personnel consultant. She brought home with her all her box files containing the stuff that related to all her areas of interest – and several carrier bags full of papers. She had an extensive 'library' of magazine articles, notes for presentations she had made and folders from courses she had attended, and was looking forward to finally having the time to develop a 'proper' filing system to keep it all in order. There had never been time at work and whenever she was asked a question about one of her specialisms she had had to go rifling through mounds of paper.

She set aside a week to devise a perfect system. The trouble was, every time she thought she'd cracked it she'd find a flaw. For instance, she put all her papers and articles about mission statements in one folder and those about in-house training

schemes in another. Then she found a magazine article about how in-house training schemes help organizations fulfill their mission statements. Where to put it? Or should she photocopy it and put a copy in each folder? She started a 'To think about later' pile. Soon this pile was bigger than all the rest and she gave up in despair.

Jane realized that while at work she'd managed very well with a simple set of box files with fairly general titles. Her real problem was that she hadn't been very good about putting papers and articles *into* the boxes promptly. So she decided to make a habit of setting aside half an hour a week to go through the pile and put everything into the most appropriate box file. It really didn't matter that the box called 'mission statements' might have some stuff that was only vaguely related – the point was Jane no longer had teetering piles of mixed papers all over her space.

# INTERRUPTIONS:
## HOW TO REDUCE THEM

The easiest way to reduce interruptions is not to have any.

This is not about refusing to speak to anyone who dares to ask you a question when you are working. It is about changing your mindset and reclassifying interruptions into:

**Type A** – part of my work
*and*
**Type B** – stopping me working

## *How many of the things you call 'interruptions' are actually a legitimate part of your job?*

### CASE STUDY

Sue was Reception Manager in a busy, small hotel. As well as taking her turn on the reception desk she supervised the other two receptionists and the three porters/maintenance staff. She organized the rotas, summarized time sheets and prepared monthly personnel returns.

On one particularly busy afternoon, Sue had just settled down to the monthly task of summarizing the time-sheets, when a man appeared at the reception desk. Angela, the duty receptionist, was temporarily away from the desk. With a big sigh, Sue approached the guest. 'I'll never get this finished if I keep getting interrupted,' she said, not quite under her breath.

Luckily, the man was a regular guest. 'Sue,' he said 'I'm not an interruption to your work – I AM your work!'

For Sue, checking in guests was a 'Type A' interruption.

# KEEP A TIME LOG FOR A WEEK

Yes it takes time, but the pay-offs can be enormous. Be as precise (and honest) as possible. Do the timekeeping as you go through the day, but save the analysis until the end of the week.

**1** Make a note of the time you start each activity.

**2** Describe what you are doing in a few words.

**3** Note the time each interruption starts, including times you interrupt yourself.
   (You will need to explain this politely to some of the other people who interrupt you.)

**4** Note the time you resume the original activity.

For example, a section of your completed time log might look like this:

**10.20** Got out papers for meeting.

**10.25** Started reading financial summary report ready for discussion at meeting.

**10.35** Fred came in with printout I needed for meeting. We clarified a couple of figures.

**10.46** Picked up report again and started reading.

**10.50** Went to water cooler for drink. Bumped into Bill and chatted about last night's game.

**11.05** Picked up report again and started reading.

**11.20** Packed up papers and left for meeting.

Without the time log you might have thought, 'I spent nearly an hour reading that financial summary report. No wonder I didn't get much else done this morning.' In fact you actually spent about 29 minutes on it, because of two interruptions. The first was a 'Type A' (Fred – 11 minutes) and the second a 'Type B' (Bill – 15 minutes). By looking at a few typical days you will be able to see how much of your time is taken up by the two types of interruption, and how much time you could save by cutting down on 'Type B interruptions'.

# REDUCE THE NUMBER OF TYPE B INTERRUPTIONS

### Drop-in visitors

How welcoming is the area immediately around your work space?

Is there an empty chair right next to your desk? This chair is saying to anyone who comes in, 'Please sit on me.'

Do you face the direction from which people approach, so that you always feel tempted to look up and smile? Your smile is saying, 'Please interrupt me – my work is less important than yours.'

If possible, rearrange your work space so that approaching people are not in your line of sight, and lose the spare chair or put it somewhere less convenient for visitors.

Of course, your job may be all about welcoming people into your space. If you are a staff welfare officer you can hardly barricade yourself in. If you are the office cashier, the cash office has to be open some of the time. But you can advertise your 'opening hours' – just make sure you stick to them so that all your colleagues get the message.

### Voicemails

Does everyone phone you rather than look things up for themselves? Are you plagued by dozens of messages every time you return to your desk?

Put a lengthy message on your answerphone or voicemail. Research has shown that most callers don't wait for the end of a long message and so don't leave a message. (This may mean that you get more phone calls when you are answering your phone, but it should cut down the amount of time you spend answering voicemails.)

# REDUCE THE LENGTH OF EACH TYPE B INTERRUPTION

Sometimes old-fashioned things work best – have an egg timer (the type with sand in) beside your phone. It's a nicely portioned piece of time and a bit less intrusive than the buzzer on your watch. Turn it over at the start of each call. You'll be surprised at how it helps you keep track of the length of your phone conversations. (If your phone has call duration display – use that.)

Use your **assertiveness** skills. When someone asks, 'Have you got a minute?' reply, 'Yes, but only a minute – I really must finish this report,' or even, 'No, not at the moment. I must finish this report. I'll pop round to see you later.'

When someone comes into your space move round to greet them – they will spend less time chatting if you have taken control and are not sitting behind your desk. (Funnily enough, it is also easier to end a phone call if you have moved away – so stand up or move your chair back.)

A final thought – how many of your colleagues' Type B interruptions are you responsible for?

# DISTRACTIONS:
## WE DO TO OURSELVES

Many people feel that they lose the ability to **concentrate** as they get older. As we have seen, it's not age that causes most of the changes in our abilities – it's our responses to other factors. At work, we may have become too busy to be in the habit of long periods of concentration, or perhaps we have lost interest or enthusiasm for the subject that we need to focus on. The good news is that everyone has the ability to concentrate deeply – we just need to harness that ability when we need it. Remember when you got completely absorbed in a book or a film or deeply engrossed in a hobby or activity. OK, so writing the minutes of the last team meeting may not be quite as much fun as helping your daughter put together her model boat, but you can use some of the same skills and achieve a similar sense of satisfaction.

Let's use the analogy of running.

## ON YOUR MARKS

Different events need different training schedules. Is the task you're facing more like a sprint or a marathon? Is it more like a solo or a team event? What equipment will you need? We can find it easy to distract ourselves from getting down to work when we haven't got ready properly.

If a piece of work is going to need you to be at the peak of your concentration, set aside time for it when you know you'll be at your best. For example, if you can't think straight until after you've had a coffee and caught up with your colleagues, wait until after that to start.

Do all you can to get the conditions right for yourself by removing the potential for outside distractions. Shut the door if you can and put your answerphone on. Make sure that your chair is comfortable – you need to have an alert but relaxed posture, with everything you need, such as a notepad, reference books or files with the relevant information, in easy reach. Make sure you have enough light and air.

Many people remember that they did their best concentrating in their student days with music playing in the background. If this would help you use a personal stereo. This has the added advantage of blocking out unwanted external distractions.

# GET SET

Now is the moment to focus on where you are going with this work:

What is the overall objective?

Are there any short- and medium-term goals?

What outcomes do you want?

Which standards will be applied?

Which skills and attributes are you going to use?

What new things will you learn along the way?

# ACTIVITY

Ask yourself the questions above about a task you have to tackle, in this instance writing up the minutes of last Friday's team meeting.

### WHAT IS THE OVERALL OBJECTIVE?

To get the minutes written and circulated by the end of this week

### ARE THERE ANY SHORT- AND MEDIUM-TERM GOALS?

- To decide on a format that's not too formal but gets all the action points down
- To get a first draft ready by the end of this morning
- To get Raj, our team leader, to read through this by the end of today so he can tell me if I'm on the right lines

### WHAT OUTCOMES DO YOU WANT?

- A move away from the overly formal style of minutes we used to have, which I don't think most of us read
- For people to think I can do a good job on this

### WHICH STANDARDS WILL BE APPLIED?

- It doesn't need to be perfect first time
- People will remember the way Joan used to do them but that's OK

### WHICH SKILLS AND ATTRIBUTES ARE YOU GOING TO USE?

- My meetings expertise from my last job
- The stuff I learned on the Plain English course last month

### WHAT NEW THINGS WILL YOU LEARN ALONG THE WAY?

- Different ways in which different team leaders like things done
- How to summarize lots of discussion into short action points

Of course, you don't have to write all this down – but doing so will certainly help you to focus. It will also help to make a daunting task seem more manageable and might even make a dull one more interesting.

# GO!

### SET YOURSELF REALISTIC TARGETS
It would be crazy for most people to say to themselves, 'I'll work at this non-stop for three hours or until I've finished.' It is much better to work for bursts of half an hour, have short breaks and come back to it feeling refreshed.

### GIVE YOURSELF A LITTLE TREAT
Reward yourself when you have achieved each of your targets. These don't need to be in the form of food or too much caffeine or nicotine. Taking a five-minute breath of air, or letting yourself read a couple of pages of your magazine would both be good ways of refreshing yourself and encouraging the creativity to flow again for the next lap.

### KEEP A DISTRACTION LIST
When something else pops into your mind, such as 'Must remember a card for Jeff', write it down on your distraction list to deal with later. Then you can forget about it and get on with your main task.

### VARY YOUR ACTIVITIES
It's not only young children who find concentrating and sitting still for long periods difficult. Try to include a variety of activities in your task – highlighting, reading, writing, walking around while thinking and so on.

### USE YOUR DISTRACTION PRODUCTIVELY
This is a useful technique when you are thinking. Notice when you have become distracted and use the distraction to make a connection with the thing that you are meant to be thinking about. For example, if when you are summarizing a presentation you attended you notice a woman walking along the street outside with a huge dog. Big dog – strength – strong arguments in favour of the subject ... and you are back on track. Don't struggle to find a connection – it doesn't matter if one doesn't come. The point is, you are soon back with your main task. In fact, this simple technique will soon become second nature and will not only help you to resist distractions, but will lead you to some good creative thinking.

# *Approach your work as a relay race, not a marathon*

# 5 POWER UP YOUR THINKING

*As we've seen, our brains work by making connections, and almost any analogy shows how important it is to remove blocks. The traffic won't flow if a car breaks down in the middle of the road. Electricity doesn't work if insulation tape is wrapped around the plug. The room gets stuffy if all the windows are shut and air can't circulate.*

## GET RID OF YOUR THINKING BLOCKS

We inadvertently put breakdowns, insulators and shut windows in the way of our thinking. Let's have a look at some of them, in order to understand and then get rid of them.

### Perceptual shut windows

How you look at something affects how well you'll be able to think about it. Is the glass half empty or half full? These are some of the ways in which failure to look at a problem with an open mind means that we can't work out what the underlying problem is, and so will not be able to solve it:

- Stereotyping, and limiting the problem too closely. For example, 'We are short-staffed because younger workers haven't got the same loyalty as older people.'
- Failure to isolate the issues. For example, 'We're short of staff and customer complaints are rising.'
- Inability to see other viewpoints. For example, 'No one likes a shop with no music in the background.'
- 'That's not logical.' What if it worked anyway?

### Emotional insulating tape

We need to be aware of our feelings in any given situation, because they can be a guide as to how best to deal with what is happening. However, feelings can block our thinking if we let them take over.

- Fear of looking silly or sounding foolish. How often have you sat in a meeting, not quite clear what's going on, but been afraid to ask?

- Fear of taking a risk. You may have got strong messages in the past about not stepping out of line.
- Anger that your values are being challenged. For example, in a discussion that seems to be heading towards a decision to reduce staff numbers, you may feel so angry on behalf of the staff that you stop evaluating what is being said.
- Excitement about a possibility. Your judgment might be clouded by the chance to do something new.

### Cultural barriers

We put these up when we have become overly sensitive about the prevailing culture – in its widest sense – so that we stop ourselves thinking 'the unthinkable'.

- Taboos. These arise when we think we can't possibly entertain certain ideas. For example, suppose you are extremely short of space in a new office. The only solution is to put Bill and Jane at the same workstation, but everyone knows they once had an affair, so we couldn't possibly …
- 'Thinking is a serious business.' We've heard: 'Quietly please, I'm thinking,' so often that anything that suggests that we might laugh or enjoy the process is too hard to take.
- 'We'd better follow the rules.' You won't be punished just for challenging the 'rules' in your mind.

### Environmental blocks

We all know what conditions we need in order to be able to think. For some it's with plenty of people around them, for others it's absolute silence. As we saw in Chapter 4 there's a lot we can do to take control of our environment. And later in this chapter, we'll look at a very specific type of 'thinking environment' to help us use our minds to their full potential.

### Intellectual breakdowns

This is all about having the tools for the task.

- Inadequate thinking techniques. Thinking isn't a subject on the curriculum of most schools or colleges, so most people don't come across the techniques – unless they get a book.
- 'I'm not really qualified to contribute on this.' Perhaps you're not in terms of job skill or experience, but the thought you contribute might be just the one needed.
- Lack of correct information. How frustrating it is to spend time thinking about an issue and sorting out a solution only to find out that one of our basic facts was wrong or incomplete. We also need to make sure that our information is based on fact and not assumptions or opinions, either our own or someone else's.
- 'I'm just not creative.' This needs challenging every time it pops up. You may not have had much practice lately, that's all.

# PROBLEM OR CHALLENGE?

The first step in thinking about an issue is to check that you're thinking about the right thing. And if you're thinking with someone else, that you agree about what the issue actually is. As an example, here's a common problem:

'The trouble is, we need more space in this office.'

Actually, what we've just done is state a solution – more space. But what would we be using that space for? You may think we need more space to give us all more shelving options, but I'm expecting to squeeze in another desk.

## REFRAMING

One great technique for finding solutions is called 'reframing'. It enables us:

**1 To get a different perspective**

It turns a problem into a challenge. All you need to do is turn the stated problem into a 'how to' statement. For example, 'We haven't got enough money to decorate the staff room,' becomes:

**How to get the funding for the redecoration** *or*
**How to reduce the cost of redecorating** *or*
**How to get materials for free** *or*
**How to get someone else to pay for it** *or*
**How to change our minds about needing it** *or*
**How to find another way to improve** *or*
**How to feel better about not doing it**

**2 To break a stalemate**

It helps us to identify as much as possible that we agree on. For example, My company needs to be paid $50 a tonne to make a profit. Your company cannot afford to pay more than $48 a tonne. **What do we have in common?** Cash limits and the need to stay in business. Let's think about:

**Other ways we can save money.**
**Providing something to make up the shortfall.**
**Providing something to reduce costs.**
**Offering some of the product to another company.**

### 3 To analyse a problem

It helps us to find out what the issues really are, making it possible to identify the positive aspects of the problem, and then see how they affect what we're really trying to do. For example, if the problem appears to be: 'This room is very dark because of the tree outside the window', it helps to identify the **positive aspects** of this situation:

**The tree is beautiful. So we're not talking about cutting it down.**
**The room is cool in the summer. So it's not an air-conditioning problem.**
**It stops people staring in. So privacy's not the issue.**
**The room is gloomy. So perhaps the issue is how to brighten the room up.**

## THE MAGIC WAND TECHNIQUE

This is another type of reframing. Firstly, imagine that your fairy godmother has waved her magic wand and your problem has been solved. What can you now do that you couldn't do before? How does the world look now?

For example:
**'I never have time to do any tidying up.'**

Imagine the magic wand doing its stuff. You now have time to do the tidying. What is the issue now? **'I have time, but I don't know where I'm going to put everything.'**

Magic wand ...

**'OK, I can see a system, but I've got too much stuff.'** Ah, all along the issue has actually been that I keep so much stuff that tidying up becomes too daunting.

## ACTIVITY

Have a go at reframing some of the problems you want to think about.
If you can't think of any right now, have a go at these:
1 No one is willing to work overtime.
2 There's not enough work in this section.
3 I can't cope with all the emails I get every day.

# THE STEPPING-STONE GUIDE T
# PROBLEM-SOLVING

*Stepping-stones across a river are usually fixed in place and order, but may not be in a straight line. So this is a helpful analogy for thinking about problem-solving.*

When solving a problem we use both the right and left brain hemispheres of our brains (see page 13). We need some **structure** and some **freedom** in order to arrive at the best, most workable solution. The following method is **logical** and **analytical** in itself and uses **creative thinking** techniques along the way. It's quite a lengthy and detailed process, and won't be appropriate in full for every problem-solving situation you face, but do try to work through it completely now.

## STEP 1 Clarify your problem

As we've seen, it's not always straightforward to work out exactly what the problem is. It is vital to make sure that the problem is actually something you want and need to tackle and that it is within your control to do something about it (even if the final decision isn't yours). For example, you probably wouldn't get very far trying to solve the problem: 'My office isn't on a Caribbean island,' however systematic a method you used.

Use the reframing techniques already mentioned to get this step right for you.

## STEP 2 Limit the scope of the problem

Are you tackling this for everyone in the company, for the next five years, or just the ten people in your office for the next six months?

## STEP 3 Analyse the causes

Why is this a problem? Draw up a list of the most likely causes. Remember to avoid preconceived notions and stereotypes.

## STEP 4 Generate possible solutions

This is where you can use a well-known creative tool called 'brainstorming' by just noting down all the ideas you come up with, no matter how mad they seem. We'll look at this in more detail in Chapter 9. For now, just remember that at this stage we're aiming to create as many ideas as possible. Resist the temptation to evaluate them at this stage and put all thoughts of resource constraints out of your mind.

## STEP 5 Set out your criteria for a successful solution

Notice that we are doing this *after* generating ideas. We are less likely to be judgmental about ideas if we haven't got preset criteria in mind. Of course, some of your criteria may well have begun to emerge as you clarified your problem. For example: 'How to get more office space so we can fit in a water cooler' implies that one criterion will be that the extra space will be a certain size.

## STEP 6 Rank and weight your criteria

Not all the criteria will be equally important, so sort out those which must be met and those which are not essential.

## STEP 7 Evaluate the solutions

Now is the time to start weighing up all the solutions you've generated. This is a fairly analytical process, but there are a few ways to do it, which we'll cover later. Two mistakes that people often make at this stage are:

- Throwing some ideas out too soon, without even measuring them against the criteria, because they sound fanciful, or 'don't feel right'. You may need to be able to justify why you *didn't* choose certain options.
- Conversely, choosing a solution by gut feeling and manipulating the criteria to fit. If this happens, it shows that you haven't thought hard enough about your criteria. For example, if you choose an option because: 'I just feel most people will like it, even though it costs more than we agreed,' then 'most people liking it' should have been a highly rated criterion. If it wasn't, it should not be the main reason for choosing a particular solution.

## STEP 8 Decide

This may not be as easy as it sounds. Yes, you've been right through the process so far and your chosen option is clearly the best. But deciding will mean letting the other possibilities go.

## STEP 9 Put the solution into practice

Depending on the size and nature of the problem you've been working on, you may need an action plan, a piloting process, target dates for the different stages and so on. Or perhaps you just get on and do it.

## STEP 10 Monitor and review progress

Again, sometimes this will be a big project in itself. But even if your decision was a simple one, if you want to keep your brain fit, it's a great idea to spend some time reviewing the thought processes you went through as you solved the problem.

**What have you learned?**
**What did you do well?**
**What would you do differently another time?**

# IMPLEMENTABILITY
## HOW TO GIVE YOUR SOLUTION A CHANCE OF WORKING

Have you ever spent ages working on a problem, come up with what you really believe to be an excellent solution and made your presentation, only to have the thing gather dust on a shelf because no one's acted on it?

Perhaps you didn't put enough 'implementability' criteria into your decision-making process.

## WHAT ARE IMPLEMENTABILITY CRITERIA?

These are the conditions that you and other people in your workplace will apply to any proposal. If it does not meet enough of them, it is just not going to happen:

- Is it politically acceptable? Is it going to go against the interests of anyone powerful enough to stop it?

- Is it organizationally consistent? Does it fit in with our usual practices, match the 'way we do things in this company'?

- Is it administratively convenient? Will the people who are actually going to be doing the work be able to?

- Is it relevant? Is the original problem important enough to the people who'll be making the final decision?

- Is it critical? Is this something on which the company gets judged?

- Is it technically feasible? It must look as though it will actually work.

# CASE STUDY

Martin was keen to organize the remodelling of the marketing office which he shared with eight other marketing people and Jan, who was secretary to Bill, the head of the department.

Twice, Martin had drawn up plans, showing how everyone would have more space when the new furniture arrived and Jan would be nearer the door, so making access easier for Bill.

Each time, Bill looked at Martin's proposals and said, 'Great, I'll run it past everyone at the next meeting.' Twice, nothing had happened.

Finally, Martin lost patience and challenged Bill, 'Look, why does nothing keep happening? You agreed we needed to make that office look smarter.'

'Yes, but you didn't ask Jan what would be best for her. You've assumed she wants to be nearer the door. In fact she doesn't want to leave the window – she reckons she's got the best view of the river in the whole building – better even than the Chairman. If Jan's not happy, I won't be.'

Martin had omitted to look at the implementabilty criteria for everyone involved.

# ACTIVITY

1 Identify something that you are having trouble getting agreement for, or a problem you're having in getting a proposal accepted.
2 Compile a list of the people or groups involved in or affected by your idea. Don't forget all those who might lose out in some way if your idea went ahead.
3 Alongside each name note the 'implementabilty' criteria they will be using to judge your idea.
4 Then list all the ways in which your idea does and doesn't match. Don't forget to check that any assumptions you might be making are, in fact, correct.

| OTHERS AFFECTED BY MY IDEA | THEIR IMPLEMENTABILTY CRITERIA | MATCH/ MISMATCH |
|---|---|---|
| | | |

# THE WHOLE PERSON MODEL FO
# PROBLEM-SOLVINC

We found out earlier that our personalities affect our thinking. Although Jung suggested that we have preferences for Sensing or INtuition, Thinking or Feeling, we are all able to use our less preferred aspects and bring them into play when we are thinking about problems.

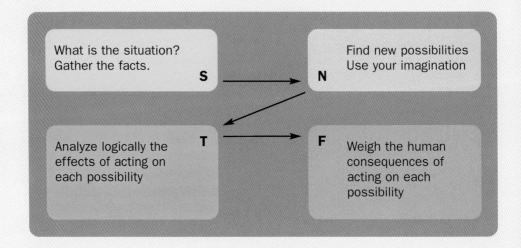

| | |
|---|---|
| What is the situation? Gather the facts. **S** | Find new possibilities Use your imagination **N** |
| Analyze logically the effects of acting on each possibility **T** | **F** Weigh the human consequences of acting on each possibility |

Use your Sensing abilities to:
- **look at the situation realistically**
- **find out exactly what's going on**
- **find out what has been tried already**

Use your iNtuition to:
- **generate all the possibilities**
- **go beyond presented facts**
- **imagine the future**

Use your Thinking to:
- **analyse cause and effect impersonally**
- **decide on the weighting and ranking of criteria**
- **look at consequences of alternative solutions**
- **match solutions to criteria**

Use your Feeling to:
- **consider others' feelings as well as your own**
- **look at the values involved**
- **consider the commitment of everyone to the solution**

# CREATING THE RIGHT THINKING CLIMATE

Creating the right thinking 'climate' is as important as having a good physical environment. Nancy Kline, founder of 'Time To Think', has been working with individuals and organizations for many years – helping them to think positively, fire up their creativity and reach better decisions. She has developed the concept of the 'thinking environment', which has ten components:

## 1 Attention

Listening with respect, interest and fascination

## 2 Incisive questions

Removing the assumptions that limit ideas

## 3 Equality

Treating each other as thinking peers
Giving equal turns and attention
Keeping agreements and boundaries

## 4 Appreciation

Practising a 5:1 ratio of appreciation to criticism

## 5 Ease

Offering freedom from rush or urgency

## 6 Encouragement

Moving beyond competition with each other

## 7 Feelings

Allowing sufficient emotional release to restore thinking

## 8 Information

Providing a full and accurate picture of reality

## 9 Place

Creating a physical environment that says to people, 'You matter'

## 10 Diversity

Adding quality because of the differences between us

# APPLYING THE TEN COMPONENTS IN THE WORKPLACE

The ten components are quite simple – but, as the case study below demonstrates, not necessarily easy.

## CASE STUDY

The meeting starts on time and the chairperson, George, settles everyone down and gets started on the first item on the agenda. He reminds everyone that the meeting must finish in three hours because the room's booked for a focus group.

Two of the people in the room are having difficulty seeing because of strong sunlight coming through a window, but they don't say anything as they don't want to make a fuss.

Most people don't have anything to contribute for the first three items on the agenda so those are dealt with quickly. Then, at item 4, everyone starts talking at once. George calls for order and tells Fred to keep quiet because we all know he has strong feelings about this issue and it would be best if he kept them to himself.

Eventually an agreement is reached about an action point, but not before Mary and John have managed to find something critical to say about every suggestion.

Tom has noticed that some of the figures in the notes are wrong anyway, but can't quite bring himself to mention it at this late stage. Luckily, at this moment a tray of coffee is brought in and everyone can focus on getting their drink while Bill drones on about an idea he's had for improving the quality of meetings.'

Does this sound familiar? Perhaps it's a bit of an exaggeration, although many meetings do seem to be rather like that. **Whose fault is it?** We often blame the person taking the chair, or the people who hijacked the discussion or perhaps the fact that no one got the documents soon enough.

In the scenario above it's fairly obvious that none of the ten components for a thinking environment was present. Do you think the people at that meeting would have been producing their best-quality ideas? Assuming they managed to agree on any actions at all, what do you think the quality would have been?

### Taking responsibility

In fact, we could all take some responsibility for creating a thinking environment in our workplace. Just altering a couple of the components would make a big difference. Imagine how much better you'd be able to think if you knew you weren't going to be interrupted or hurried along.

## THINKING ENVIRONMENT AUDIT

Think of one of your typical work situations. It could be a meeting, formal or informal, an appraisal session with one of your staff or your manager or a discussion with colleagues about a new system – anything that seems relevant and useful to you.

1  Look again at the ten components and identify any that are already present in the situation. For example, 'Equality: We all get a turn to speak at our weekly project meeting and are encouraged to say how the project's going for us.'

2  Identify any that are not present. For example, 'Encouragement. We all seem to want to outdo each other moaning about how tough it is. We don't really listen.'

3  Think what you can do to remedy this. Aim for an action that you will feel able to take to allow that component to happen. For example, 'Next meeting I'll ask my colleague to say a bit more about their experience and not jump in with mine.'

## *How productive are the meetings you attend?*

## *Does everyone leave the meeting with a sense of achievement?*

## *What could you do to create a better thinking environment?*

# MOTIVATION
# MATTERS

*People who are inspired to think and work in ways that produce the best results will be tapping into their own motivational forces.*

Motivational theories start with the assumption that given the chance and the right stimuli, people work well and positively.

The management psychologist, A. H. Maslow, suggests that these stimuli can be grouped into five areas:

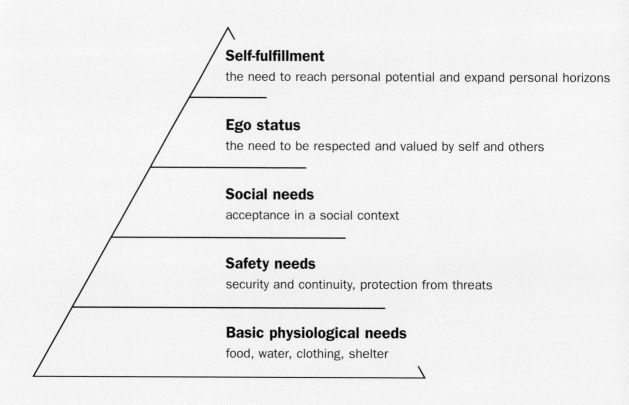

**Self-fulfillment**
the need to reach personal potential and expand personal horizons

**Ego status**
the need to be respected and valued by self and others

**Social needs**
acceptance in a social context

**Safety needs**
security and continuity, protection from threats

**Basic physiological needs**
food, water, clothing, shelter

We will find it hard to operate at each higher level unless we have met the needs of the one below. And of course, our needs change throughout our working life. You may have been very motivated by the sports facilities (allowing your social needs to be met) when you started work, but now with children to think about your needs may have changed. Now, 'acceptance' means something different – perhaps an acknowledgment that you are still committed to your job, even though you can't join in sports events after work.

# Given the chance and the right stimuli, people work well and positively

Employers and managers have to recognize that people's needs do change over time, and that each individual's needs are different. This is important if you are a manager.

Suppose your company is planning to move its head office across the country to the same town as its main production facility. Everyone has been assured that this is not a cost-cutting exercise with redundancies to follow. You think this is an exciting opportunity for you and your partner to move out of your flat into a house. Most of your team are also keen for different reasons. But one person is very concerned. They've just spent a difficult few months getting their elderly mother into a suitable retirement home nearby. They don't want to give up this job, and travelling back every weekend will be too expensive.

Think how demotivated they are likely to be – and the effect of this on their ability to think clearly about their work. It won't be any help to them to say, 'Come on, just have a positive mental attitude.'

Using what we've done so far in this chapter, what could you do to help this person?

**a) as their manager**
**b) as their colleague**

For example, how would you help them to clarify the actual problem, and generate solutions.

# GETTING YOUR THINKING
# OBJECTIVES CLEAR

*We've already looked at making sure we're thinking about the right problem and how to avoid limiting our thinking by assuming that we know what the solution is.*

We do, however, need to make sure that we're heading in the right general direction. It would be a waste of time taking part in a working party to devise a new strategy for improving customer service, only to discover that another group was working on reducing customer contact time.

When you have an appraisal or annual review you probably set your work objectives for the next year. You may find the acronym **SMART** useful when setting these objectives, to make sure they are:

**S**pecific  **M**easurable  **A**greed  **R**ealistic  **T**ime-limited

In contrast, your 'thinking objectives' also need to be **CRISP**:

| | |
|---|---|
| **C**onstructive | *Avoid negative, limiting language* |
| **R**ough direction | *Provide a general framework rather than strict tramlines* |
| **I**nvolving | *Something worth working on* |
| **S**uitable | *Generally in line with the business and work objectives* |
| **P**rincipled | *Fit in with your values* |

If you have ever found yourself feeling rather half-hearted about something, not really wanting to take part, it maybe that the objective wasn't **CRISP** enough. For example, 'Come up with a strategy for improving service to telephone customers, while not increasing contact time' would be a **CRISP** objective:

| | |
|---|---|
| **C**onstructive | *No negative, limiting words* |
| **R**ough direction | *Doesn't tell us how to do it, leaves us free to think widely* |
| **I**nvolving | *Yes, I feel this is worth me devoting some energy to* |
| **S**uitable | *Fits overall business strategy of improvement and cost control* |
| **P**rincipled | *It's right to treat customers well, it's right not to waste time* |

On the other hand, 'Come up with a way of cutting the time we spend with each customer, without them knowing what we're up to', is not a **CRISP** objective, as it implies some dishonesty and 'cutting' sounds more negative than 'improving'.

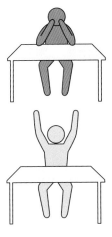

## ACTIVITY: MOTIVATION CHECK

**1** Think of a time you felt demotivated at work.

What was it about the situation, those around you and you yourself that contributed to your demotivation?

Which of your needs was not being met?

How **CRISP** were your objectives?

**2** Now, think of a time when you felt highly motivated at work.

What was it about the situation, those around you and you yourself that contributed to your motivation?

Where were you on the list of needs?

Did you have **CRISP** objectives to help you?

**3** Think about how motivated you are now at work.

What could you do to raise your motivation if necessary and maintain it?

# HOW TO REVIVE FLAGGING MOTIVATION

**1** Have a break. Changing your activity won't stop the flow but you will return to the task feeling refreshed. A change of environment will help even more. It may not actually be the cup of tea that invigorates you – it may be the few minutes you spend standing in the staff room waiting for the kettle to boil.

**2** Give yourself a pat on the back. Look back over what you've done so far and make yourself notice all the good points.

**3** Give yourself a tangible reward – something that will improve your mood, and not induce guilt. So, if you are watching your weight, an extra portion of chips might not be a good reward, but promising yourself a candle-lit bath might be.

**4** Find a way to break up what you're doing into chunks. If you already have, find a different way. For example, if you are writing a report you might be doing it in sections according to who provided each category of information. So, try breaking it up into chunks that are each of a certain number of words.

**5** Do some physical exercise. Even a few minutes will improve your circulation and you might find a new solution comes while you're doing it.

**6** Try a creative way of looking at what you're doing. How is your task like sailing a ship, for example? How would you be working if you travelled back in time a hundred years? Or forward a hundred years?

# 6 MAKE THE MOST OF YOUR MEMORY

*Everything we do involves our memories. We cannot think without accessing our memory and all the unconscious things we do, like walking or holding a cup, rely on the memory of how we did it last time. And yet many people believe they have a poor memory. For example, the woman who leaves her umbrella on the train will be irritated with herself for her forgetfulness, yet as an accountant she works with huge amounts of financial information all day. The man who forgets to pick up the dry cleaning will give himself a hard time about his bad memory – despite the fact he's a teacher.*

In reality, we all cope with huge amounts of **new information** and perform amazing memory functions every day. In addition, because our brain capacity is so under-used, there's no reason why we shouldn't capitalize on it and increase our **memory powers**. As your memory improves, you'll begin to be able to process even more information, see the bigger picture and improve your confidence.

The trouble is, for many of us, using our memory is inextricably linked to stressful situations like exams or punishment at school for forgetting to do some homework. We may still get negative comments about our memory which simply reinforce our own self-critical view.

## *Your memory is better than you think*

# HOW MEMORY WORKS

There are two elements to our memory:

**fixing something into the memory**
**recalling it when we need it again**

These are, in fact, complex processes, which involve many parts of the brain working almost simultaneously.

When we sense something (hear a telephone number, smell a rose, touch a coffee cup, and so on) an electrochemical pathway is laid down along the neurons from the site of the sense to the brain and across the synapses between them. The synapse is the minute gap between two neurons. There are 10 million billion possible connections, and each pathway is potentially a memory. The more a particular pathway is activated, the more likely it is that a memory will be created.

# TYPES OF MEMORY

We have two sorts of memory – **explicit** and **implicit**.

The **implicit** memory uses well-worn neurological pathways to enable us to do familiar things time after time.

The **explicit** memory is for the things we have to remember consciously. For example, when you ring a restaurant to book a table, your **implicit** memory tells you how to use the telephone, and your **explicit** memory reminds you what time you need to book for.

Feelings play an important part. We produce the chemicals adrenaline and noradrenaline when we undergo emotions and these act as transmitters. This partially explains why we are able to remember very clearly some things that happened at highly emotional times. So if you think about an achievement you are particularly proud of, such as winning an award, you may well be able to remember very clearly what you were wearing, what the weather was like that day and the face of the first person you told. Unfortunately, of course, the same is true for memories associated with more negative emotions.

# WHAT HAPPENS
## WHEN MEMORY FAILS ?

As emotion and stress increase, the adrenal glands work harder in order to get your body ready for its 'fight or flight' response, in whatever form that will take. The gland produces cortisol, which decreases the effectiveness of the neural connections, and so stops the memory working effectively.

This explains why we have more difficulty remembering the details of events when we were feeling panicky or highly emotional. Even Oscar-winners, well-used to public performances, report that they cannot remember what they said in their acceptance speech and that the actual ceremony is a blur.

## *"Everything happened so quickly, I can't remember much about it ..."*

## STUDYING MEMORY

Ironically, psychologists learn most about how memory works by studying people whose memories have stopped functioning properly, in the same way that an electrician can work out which way current is flowing in a complicated set of circuits when one bulb goes out.

Some conditions such as Parkinson's and Alzheimer's diseases are associated with chemical deficits, which mean that certain connections can no longer be made between neurons. Moreover, because we use different parts of the brain for different types of memory, people with such diseases, or who have lost part of their brain through accident, illness or surgery, may forget their name but can still play the violin. So the 'circuits' in the brain can be traced and studied.

# CAN WE BELIEVE
## OUR MEMORY ?

*Assuming that your memory isn't impaired by illness, injury or surgery, how reliable is it?*

## ACTIVITY

Imagine a coin or banknote. Draw both sides of it from memory in the space below.

Now get out the real thing. Have you remembered it well?

Of course, we don't need to carry an accurate description of a coin around in our heads because we can rely on the fact that we'll recognize one next time we see it. But what if we've witnessed a crime or an accident? Would we be reliable witnesses?

## IT'S ALL RELATIVE

There are many factors which affect how we remember things. In one experiment, people were asked to draw a sketch map of their country with lines showing the relative distances between cities. In their own areas the lines were always too long, and the farther away on the map they went the shorter they became relative to the correct length. Why? Were the participants exaggerating the relative importance of their own area, or did they simply feel more confident in their knowledge nearer to home?

## *Why do people have different memories of the same event?*

# SHORT-TERM
## MEMORY

*Up until the 1950s scientists thought we just had one mechanism for memory. Everything went in and the brain stored as much as it could. Now we know that the brain uses several methods to remember information in different ways and for differing lengths of time.*

Our short-term memories deal with two sorts of facts:
- **the trivia of life, such as the colour of shoes worn by the woman in the lift this morning**
- **the information we need for a brief period to carry out a specific task, but which then becomes irrelevant**

Try multiplying 39 by 8 in your head. You should get the answer of 312. Maybe you first multiplied 9 by 8 (72) and had to hold the 72 in your mind until you'd worked out 3 multiplied by 8 (24), which you then multiplied by 10 (240). Then you added the 72 (312). Once you'd got the answer, you could forget the 72.

Information from each sense is processed differently (see pages 16–17). This explains why we can do more than one task at once – as long as they don't need the same short-term memory pathways. For example, you can drive and talk to a passenger but you will have difficulty talking to someone on the phone at the same time as speaking to someone at your desk.

## HOW DOES THE SHORT-TERM MEMORY WORK?

The short-term memory has three distinct mechanisms:
- **the phonological loop, which handles sounds and words**
- **the visuo-spatial sketchpad, which registers images**
- **the central executive, which co-ordinates the others into a single thought**

### The phonological loop

The phonological loop works in two parts – a memory store and a rehearsal system. A speech-based memory trace will survive for only a couple of seconds unless the rehearsal system is used to reinforce it.

**TRY THIS EXPERIMENT**
Read each of the following sequences out loud. After reading each one, cover it up and recite it again from memory.

A **hit, can, dog, toe, hit**
B **ban, hat, map, cat, ban**

You probably found A easier than B, because sound is a factor and B had more similar-sounding words. Experiments show that success ranges from 80 per cent for A to 10 per cent for B.

**NOW TRY THESE**
C **huge, big, great, wide, large**
D **old, late, cool, fat, good**

Most people find that their results for C and D are similar, showing that meaning does not have as much effect on short-term memory as sound.

**LASTLY, HAVE A GO AT THESE**
E **opportunity, pneumonia, chancellor, refrigerator, organization**
F **hope, mumps, school, green, side**

Here, the main factor is length, and you probably found E much harder than F. Your memory of 'opportunity' will have begun to decay before you got through 'organization'.

### Visual memory trace

Have you ever made a figure 8, or your initials, in the air with a sparkler or other light point, such as a bright flashlamp? And when you go to the cinema, what you're actually seeing is a series of still images run through the projector, which you see as movement. Our brains hold each image for a fraction of a second until we see the next one. This demonstrates an aspect of our short-term memory that was first discovered in 1740 by a Swedish scientist, Segner. He measured the VMT to be about one tenth of a second.

## The digit span

This is the first scientific test of short-term memory, devised in 1887. See how you get on.

Read aloud the first line of digits, once only, at the rate of about one digit a second. Then close your eyes and repeat the sequence. If you get it right, move down to the first line with five digits. Carry on doing this until you make a mistake. Continue until you reach a length at which you are always wrong. (If you need to, add extra lines of 11, 12 and so on at the bottom.)

8 3 1 9
6 9 2 7
4 8 5 1
9 3 4 1 7
6 8 2 5 9
3 7 1 8 6
8 6 5 1 4 9
2 7 1 8 9 4
4 3 8 1 7 2
7 5 8 6 9 4 3
5 2 1 9 8 3 7
1 7 5 8 6 4 2
2 7 5 4 6 3 9 8
9 6 3 7 5 2 1 4
7 2 9 1 5 3 4 6
6 8 3 2 5 9 4 7 1
4 1 9 7 3 8 2 5 6
8 4 2 1 6 5 9 7 3
9 4 1 7 4 6 5 2 3 8
7 3 4 2 9 1 7 6 8 5
3 8 1 9 5 4 1 7 6 2

Your 'span' is the longest sequence you can recall. The average is six or seven digits. What this experiment shows is that time is the limiting factor. If you get to the end of the line before the memory of the first digit has faded, you'll probably remember the whole sequence. If you don't, you'll forget it. So, it follows that one way of improving your memory of numbers is to increase the speed at which you read them.

If you put the digits into groups of three and say them rhythmically, as a rap, this will help. So next time you want to remember a telephone number just rap it a few times.

# LONG-TERM
## MEMORY

*We probably do remember much, much more than we recall. We think we've forgotten something: what was the name of our geography teacher all those years ago? We struggle to remember and then give up. Perhaps weeks later we come across an old photo of a school geography trip and the teacher's name pops into our mind. Context is very helpful to long-term memory.*

We forget different things at different rates. Research has shown that our memory of names and faces declines fairly steadily over the first 30 years, with a rapid fall off over the next 15 years. Academic learning suffers rapid early loss, but has much more robust long-term retention. The factors involved seem to be:

- **the vividness of the original experience**
- **the frequency with which we subsequently recall it**
- **our own ageing process**
- **'interference' – when the memory of a more recent event muddles or replaces the original memory. For example, even if you go to the theatre infrequently, you may have clear memories of your last visit a few months ago. If you go to the supermarket once a week you may remember your last visit, but the rest will merge into one another and be a blur.**

As with our short-term memory, it appears that there is more than one process and mechanism involved.

### Episodic mcmory

This is where we record **past events**. Most people remember very little from before the age of five and almost nothing from before they are three. This is probably because the brain is not mature enough to lay down specific memories, but may also have something to do with our language being undeveloped. Episodic memory is one of the most fragile and easily lost.

### Semantic memory

This is where we store our **background knowledge** of the world. It reminds you what a car is and your best friend's name.

Episodic and semantic memories depend on each other but use different parts of the brain, which is why degenerative diseases may impair one and leave the other untouched.

# TEST YOUR SEMANTIC MEMORY:

In the list below, cover up the column of letters on the right.
Read quickly through the names of countries. Cross out the ones whose capital cities you know immediately and those you are sure you don't know.
Now concentrate on remembering the capital cities of the ones you think you ought to know but can't quite remember.

| | |
|---|---|
| NORWAY | O |
| TURKEY | A |
| KENYA | N |
| URUGUAY | M |
| TIBET | L |
| AUSTRALIA | C |
| SAUDI ARABIA | R |
| ROMANIA | B |
| BULGARIA | S |
| SOUTH KOREA | S |
| SYRIA | D |
| CYPRUS | N |
| SUDAN | K |
| NICARAGUA | M |
| ECUADOR | Q |
| COLOMBIA | B |
| THAILAND | B |
| VENEZUELA | C |

If you can't get them all, uncover the list of initial letters. That will probably jog your memory. (The answers are on page 139.) The feeling that something's on the tip of your tongue usually means that you do know it and all it takes is a trigger to release the memory. The trick is to find the right trigger and this is covered later in this chapter.

## Procedural memory

This is our unconscious awareness of how to do things. It is the most durable of our memory processes, and even people with serious episodic memory loss will still remember, for example, how to play the piano.

## Prospective memory

This is the memory of things you have to do in the future. It is fairly fragile as it is the one least likely to be triggered by an accidental reminder. For example, a smell might take you back to an episode in the past, but won't take you forward.

# TECHNIQUES
## FOR BETTER RECALL

### Motivation

We have looked at motivation in an earlier chapter, but it's worth reiterating here. How much you want and need to remember something plays a vital part in how willing you'll be to commit it to memory. However, just saying something is important doesn't make it stick – the motivation is about how much effort you are prepared to put into the process.

So when you really want to remember something – try out some of the memory techniques in this section. Don't just hope it will happen. As we know from other areas of life, wishing something doesn't make it happen.

### How long it takes to learn something

Experiments have shown time and again that short bursts of activity help something to stick in the memory better and for longer. We may feel we know this from experience, when a last minute 'cram' before an exam seemed to tell us more than all those weeks of sitting in a hot classroom. The trouble is, cramming isn't an activity that actually helps long-term recall on its own. Most of what you learned in a panic the night before will be gone as soon as the exam is over. Long-term recall needs short periods of high quality activity.

If you have something to learn and remember, avoid sitting at it for hours at a stretch – make a plan, do a part at a time and take breaks.

### Physiological arousal or alertness

Our alertness is lowest when we are in deep sleep and highest when we are in panic or high stress. The optimum for most activity is somewhere in between, and it may differ from one activity to another.

Work out when you are at your most comfortably alert. Things which don't need you to be thinking at your best can be done at other times – save this quality time for your most important thinking to make sure that what you need to remember goes into your long-term memory.

### Early or late?

For a long time it was assumed that the best learning happens in the morning, and indeed most school timetables are still weighted in this way. Recent experiments threw doubt on this, though, when groups of schoolchildren were told stories in the morning and afternoon and then tested on what they remembered. The groups who had heard the story in the morning did better in immediate tests, but the groups who had heard the story in the afternoon did better in tests given several days later.

The following techniques work to improve various aspects of memory, and some may suit you better than others. Try to persevere with those that seem difficult at first; they are probably related to the aspects of your memory that you want to work with.

# PATTERNS AND FRAMEWORKS – MNEMONICS

Rote learning really only works in a framework – our maths tables would be much harder to chant if 6 x 9 didn't follow right after 5 x 9. And frameworks and patterns reinforce the neurological pathways in our brains and so make the memories stronger. This fact leads to a range of techniques which can be very helpful when you need to remember details, facts, sequences and so on. A mnemonic is any device designed to help your memory. Once you get good at using them they take a lot longer to describe than to put into practice. And remember, you are motivated.

### A walk round the house

Probably the first person to use mnemonics was the Greek poet Simonides in the sixth century BC, and many people who perform amazing memory stunts today still use the method credited to him. This one is useful if you want to remember a list of things. You only have to do the initial work once, but you do need to spend some time on it so that it's well lodged in your memory. You can revisit it even when you don't have a list to remember.

#### HERE'S HOW IT WORKS

Conjure up a strong mental picture of your house, apartment or wherever you live. In your mind's eye, walk through it, stopping at ten places on your journey. Make as rich a picture as possible of each of the places. Stand and have a good look round in your mind. What colours do you see? What do you hear in each place? Don't worry if you don't have ten rooms, as long as you can identify ten separate locations.

Make sure you are clear about the route – you're going to use the same one every time you want to commit something to memory. Just to make sure, imagine yourself going back out of your house, retracing your steps.

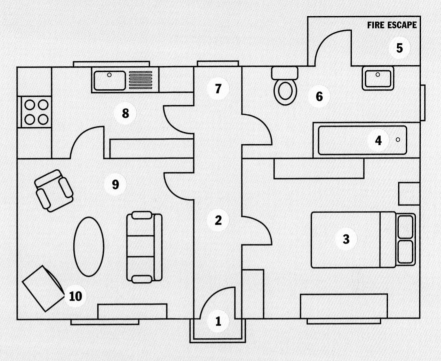

Now, suppose you want to remember ten things that you have to buy on your way home.

Imagine each item in its place in turn along your walk. Make the item memorable in some way. So you might put an enormous carrot doing a dance on the porch step, an immaculately neat pile of peas in the hall, a giant tomato tucked up in your bed, snoring loudly or a bunch of bananas taking a shower in your bathroom.

Then, when you're at the market, take the walk around your house and all the items on your list will come readily to mind.

If you have fewer than ten things to remember, just go on part of the walk (but always start at the same point). If you have more than ten to commit to memory, just go round again.

You can also use this technique to remember important things about particular aspects of your work. For example, you could make the stairs the area which is always associated with your management activities. Then, whenever you need to remember something to do with your role as a manager you imagine putting a picture of that thing on the wall of the staircase. When you've completed the activity, you can visualize yourself taking the picture down. In the same way, you can assign other work areas to other locations. Be as imaginative as you can – the more vivid the image the better the memory trace.

### Pegwords

This is a similar idea, but uses a list of ten memorable words, instead of places in your house, as 'pegs' on which to hang the things you want to remember. What you do is think of ten words that rhyme with the numbers one to ten. Again, once you've got your list sorted you'll use it a lot, so spend some time on this. It's best to have tangible nouns, rather than concepts or adjectives, because things are so much easier to visualize.

For example: one/sun; two/glue; three/tree; four/door; five/hive; six/bricks; seven/hen; eight/plate; nine/pine; ten/pen. (You can think of your own words if you prefer.)

Make your list as vivid as you can – you want it to stick.

Then, when you have a list of items to remember, you associate each item with a number word. Again make each image as ridiculous as you can – a rocket shaped carrot zooming towards the sun, peas overflowing from a huge gluepot and so on.

### Crazy headlines

The two previous techniques are mainly visual. Here's one that's verbal. It was designed by a nineteenth-century headmaster, Brayshaw, who wanted a way to help his pupils remember all the dates which history lessons of that era required. You can use it for any number, such as office security codes and PINs, and although it looks a bit daunting at first, it doesn't take long to master.

Brayshaw removed the vowels from the alphabet and set out a code for the digits from 1 to 0.

| 1 | 2 | 3 | 4 | 5 | 6 | 7 | 8 | 9 | 0 |
|---|---|---|---|---|---|---|---|---|---|
| B | D | G | J | L | M | P | R | T | W |
| C | F | H | K | S | N | Q | Z | V | X |

**Office security code? Harry Doesn't Take Many Parrots: 32967**
**Bank PIN? My Mum is a Jumping Giraffe: 6643**

## Acronyms

This technique also uses initial letters but this time you take the initial letters of the actual things you want to remember and make a word from them. We've already used at least two – **SMART** and **CRISP** objectives. An acronym doesn't have to be an actual word – a pronounceable nonsense word will do. 'ROYGBIV', pronounced as it looks, is a good way of remembering the colours of the rainbow (red, orange, yellow, green, blue, indigo and violet). This technique can be used just as easily for remembering who attends which meeting, and who should get copies of the minutes. For example, say the people who attend the weekly budget meeting are Anne, Bob, Henry, Steve and Tim, you could remember them with the acronym BATHS.

## Nonsense phrases

The initials can equally be used as the initial letters for words in a nonsense phrase. Another easy way to recall the rainbow's colours might be: 'Richard Of York Gave Battle In Vain', and you could remember who should be at the meeting with: 'All Bears Hate Squishy Tomatoes'.

## Verbalization

As we've seen, the more vivid and engaging we can make an experience, the better we'll be able to remember it.

If you need to remember a sequence of events (the series of steps needed to process a customer application, for example) don't just read through the task instructions a few times. When you actually have a go, talk it through to yourself out loud. (If you are surrounded by colleagues, mutter.) An even better way to help you remember is to teach someone else to do it. Or if no one is willing to be your pupil, imagine that you are writing out a set of desk instructions for someone who is going to take over your work while you are away.

## Remembering the names of people you meet

This is an area where many people feel vulnerable. You are introduced to someone, and the instant they turn away you've forgotten their name. Someone approaches you at a conference, and you can remember that you've seen them before, but what was their name? It's worse if they start talking as though they obviously haven't forgotten your name.

The truth is, like every other aspect of improving your memory, you have to want it to happen. It may be that some people seem to be able to remember names without any effort, but in fact they are simply at the level of unconscious competence with this, and they will be using a method of memorizing names, without realizing it.

**Follow these steps to improve your ability to remember people's names:**

**Step 1** Choose to respect this person by learning their name.
**Step 2** Listen when you're given the name. It's so easy to be focused on the handshake, worrying about how *you* look that their name has come and gone before you've started concentrating.
**Step 3** Make sure that you hear their name properly. (Ask them to spell it if it's essential for you to get it perfect.)
**Step 4** Imagine the name written down. Just doing this forces you to listen to it – many people are amazed to discover that they are suddenly good at remembering names just by doing this.
**Step 5** Visualize the name. Perhaps it sounds like the name of a famous person, or perhaps the surname is a profession, or town, or something else that you can use to make a visual image in your mind. The picture doesn't have to illustrate the whole name, just enough to act as a trigger. Involve the actual person in front of you in the image, so that the name and their face are linked.

## Recalling 'hard-to-get-at' memories

Sometimes, a memory just doesn't seem to want to surface. Techniques used to help eyewitnesses in criminal investigations can also help in everyday situations, such as remembering where you left a file of documents.

**1** Recreate the original conditions in your mind.
   How did you feel? What was the temperature like? Were you tired, energetic or hungry at the time?
**2** Concentrate on the details, even if they seem unimportant.
   If, in thinking your way around the route you took with the file before you lost it, you notice a detail like a large plant, concentrate on that for a moment. It may bring other helpful images to mind.
**3** Visualize a remembered scene from another point of view.
   Imagine that you are standing on the windowsill outside one of the offices looking in, for example. What do you see?
**4** Replay a memory in reverse.
   Visualize the room before you came into it. What happened before that ... and before that?

# THE MEMORY
# GYM

Here are some exercises and other things you can do to keep your memory in good shape.

## Basic equipment – the physical components

If you're thinking you like the sound of this gym more than the sort with the treadmills and weights – bad luck. Studies of the relationship between physical fitness and mental ability show that exercise can boost mental capacity by about 25 per cent. Even if you prefer not to do a lot of exercise, it's worth regularly checking your hearing and eyesight. A surprisingly high number of people overlook these basics.

Also, have a look at any medication you are taking. Of course, many conditions need regular drugs, but think about whether you have noticed any dulling of mental function while on a course of drugs. Sometimes it can be gradual, and it might be worth talking to your doctor about changing a prescription. Don't take any action concerning drug treatments without talking to your doctor.

## Gentle warm-up

Sit comfortably and bring to mind your 'walk around the house' or 'pegwords'.

Here's a shopping list of ten items. Use one of the recall tools above to learn them.

**Biscuits**
**Washing powder**
**Bananas**
**Potatoes**
**Postage stamps**
**Eggs**
**Juice**
**Cheese**
**Bread**
**String**

## Pay attention

- Make a conscious decision that you are going to remember things.
- When someone starts talking to you, make the effort to listen and turn off your own inner tapes.
- When you park your car in an unfamiliar car park, look around for a landmark.
- When you take a new route look out for things that you will be able to recognize on the way back, remembering they'll be on the other side then and will look slightly different.
- When you watch a film or read a book make a conscious effort to notice key points throughout and take the time at the end to recall them.

## Another list

This time, make up a sentence with words beginning with the initial letters of the Sun and planets.

**Sun**
**Mercury**
**Venus**
**Earth**
**Mars**
**Jupiter**
**Saturn**
**Uranus**
**Neptune**
**Pluto**

*What were the items on the shopping list, again?*

## Be a child again

Before you went to school and began to get tense about your memory, you didn't have any hang-ups about whether there was a right or wrong way to learn to do things. Aim to do at least one of these childlike things every day:

- **use all of your senses**
- **ask lots of questions**
- **stay positive and enthusiastic**
- **get engrossed in something**
- **try lots of ways of doing something, even if the first way works**
- **let your imagination run free**

## More to remember

Learn this list of budget codes (try using crazy headlines):

| | |
|---|---|
| **Travel expenses** | **69421** |
| **Hotel accommodation** | **69437** |
| **Stationery** | **48115** |
| **Books and periodicals** | **47218** |
| **Boardroom hospitality** | **68226** |
| **Flowers and plants** | **68905** |

*Write out the list of planets and the shopping list again.*

## Carry first aid

Don't be embarrassed about using your organizer, alarm clock, diary, tape recorder or even a humble notebook. Writing down a number, name or list can free your mind to think of something else. You do need to remember to use these aids consistently, though, and keep them handy. Don't forget that another person can be a very useful memory aid – sharing information and even getting them to remind you about certain things. Their memory might be strong in different ways to yours and this in itself might lead to all sorts of creative possibilities.

## Lists again

How many of the countries and their capital cities from page 76 can you remember?

*Now write out the other three lists you have been learning.*

# REVIEW

It would be a shame to waste all that motivation by failing to review your memory and finding it empty at the crucial moment. If you'd spent a lot of money planting your garden, you wouldn't expect to be able to leave it alone for weeks, or even days, and to come back to find it still in good condition. Get into the habit of going over things that you know you need to remember.

# 7 DEALING WITH STRESS

*We tend to equate stress with overwork, being too rushed and having a lot on our plates. In fact, not having enough to do can also lead to stress and its associated symptoms because we need a certain amount of stress to function effectively. Strictly speaking, the definition of stress is neutral: 'the system of forces applied to a structure'. Without the right amount of stress, a structure such as a bridge would either collapse or explode – the stress keeps it together.*

## WHAT IS STRESS?

In human terms, stress has been described as 'unpleasant over- or understimulation'. The word 'unpleasant' is important here because each of us has a level of optimum stress at which we are able to perform effectively and, when things are going well, a certain amount of extra challenge can even be invigorating. For example, if you are in a job that depends on the needs of customers, you're likely to feel all right as long as customers present themselves in a steady stream, and you are able to deal with their requests. But you'll probably feel stressed if there aren't any customers or if there are just too many to deal with in the time you have available, although the stress may present itself in different ways.

### How does stress manifest itself?

Stress shows itself in various ways: physical symptoms, emotional signals and changes in our behaviour. The easiest signs to spot are the physical ones like:
- **headaches**
- **upset stomach**
- **palpitations**
- **skin complaints**
- **neck and back pain**

but we often disregard these, or associate them with some cause other than stress.

# THE THREE LEVELS OF STRESS AND HOW THEY AFFECT OUR PERFORMANCE

## 1 NOT ENOUGH GOING ON: 'UNDER STRESS'

**Feelings:**
bored
demotivated
restless
lethargic

**Performance:**
distracted easily
keep putting things off
get preoccupied with unimportant details
low production

## 2 THE RIGHT AMOUNT GOING ON: 'OPTIMUM STRESS'

**Feelings:**
energy
excitement
confidence and optimism
motivation
high self-esteem

**Performance:**
sound judgment
logical thinking
creative thinking
high production

## 3 TOO MUCH GOING ON: 'OVER STRESS'

**Feelings:**
irritability
fatigue
overwhelmed
close to tears
loss of perspective

**Performance:**
forgetfulness
lack of concentration
irrational decisions
poor communication

# HOW STRESS AFFECTS
# OUR THINKING

*Many of us are aware that stress affects our ability to think – either for better or worse. Just after an accident, we seem to be able to see exactly what needs to be done and wonder afterwards how we coped. On the other hand, think of the first few panicky moments of an exam, when the questions seem to be written in a foreign language. Now scientists are beginning to explain just what is going on.*

The production of adrenaline helps us physically in the short term. Our hearts beat up to five times faster, our blood vessels expand to allow more blood to circulate and our pupils dilate. We're ready for action. But too much adrenaline and its associated hormone, cortisol, can have a negative effect on the brain, shrinking the hippocampus and destroying neurons.

Recent tests have shown that cortisol, in particular, may be associated with memory loss. Volunteers were given lists of words and asked to recall them after a short time. Some of the people had previously been put through stressful experiences, like speaking in public for five minutes or counting backwards in steps of 17 (remembering lists of words can be stress-inducing in itself). The people who simply had to remember the words, without the other tests, did better than the others and the women better than the men. It looks as if women and men are affected differently by cortisol.

## STRESS AND COMPETENCE

As we've seen, the higher up the competence ladder we go the less effort we need to devote to thinking about what we're doing. It seems that when we undergo stress, those unconscious thought pathways are blocked, even if only temporarily, and we move back down the ladder a step, or even two. We become more mechanical in what we do and more conscious of having to think about it.

In fact, we may think too much about what we're doing. We become like the tightrope walker with a sudden attack of nerves, who starts thinking about how far away the ground actually is. She would need someone to talk her through all her moves so that she could safely get back. If she actually gets to a state of panic, she can't function at all. The short-term memory of how to perform is lost – and she might find herself in the safety net.

# THE STRESS
## WE CAUSE OURSELVES

When we were children, we learned how the world worked by watching and listening to the people around us. They gave us a set of values that they believed would help us to get on in our lives. For example, 'It's a good thing to help other people, and people will like you if you're helpful.' I doubt if anyone would argue with that. The trouble is that our most strongly held beliefs and values can get out of perspective when we are stressed and drive us to behave in ways which are unhelpful to us, and give us even more stress.

## STRESS QUESTIONNAIRE

Try this simple questionnaire to find out which if any of the five 'stress drivers' you have and how they affect you.

Answer each question 'yes', 'no' or 'sometimes'.

**A**

Do you set yourself high standards and then get annoyed with yourself when you don't meet them?

Is it important for you to be right?

Do you feel annoyed or irritated by small messes such as a spot on your clothes, or discrepancies like an ornament or tool out of place, or minor errors in a piece of work?

Do you hate to be interrupted?

Do you like to explain things in detail and precisely?

**B**

Do you do things (especially for others) that you don't really want to do?

Is it important for you to be liked?

Are you fairly easily persuaded?

Do you dislike being 'different'?

Do you dislike conflict?

**C**

Do you tend to do a lot of things at the same time?

Do you find yourself getting impatient with others?

Do you have a tendency to talk at the same time as others, or finish their sentences for them?

Do you like to 'get on with the job' rather than talk about it?

Do you set unrealistic time limits (especially too short)?

**D**

Do you hide or control your feelings?

Are you reluctant to ask for help?

Do you tend to put yourself (or find yourself) in the position of being depended upon?

Do you tend not to realize how tired, or hungry, or ill you are, but instead 'keep going'?

Do you prefer to do things on your own?

**E**

Do you hate 'giving up' or 'giving in', always hoping that this time it will work?

Do you have a tendency to start things and not to finish them?

Do you tend to compare yourself (or your performance) with others and feel inferior or superior accordingly?

Do you find yourself going round in circles with a problem, feeling stuck but unable to let go of it?

Do you have the tendency to be the 'rebel' or 'odd one out' in a group?

# SCORING

Score 1 point for 'yes', ½ a point for 'sometimes' and 0 for 'no'. Add up your score for each of the five sections, which relate to the stress drivers below.

| Question | Score | Driver |
|---|---|---|
| A | | 'Be perfect' driver |
| B | | 'Please' driver |
| C | | 'Hurry up' driver |
| D | | 'Be strong' driver |
| E | | 'Try hard' driver |

A score of three or more in any section indicates a tendency toward that particular driver. Most people experience all the drivers at different times, but generally have two or three drivers that crop up regularly.

# THE VALUES UNDERPINNING THE FIVE DRIVERS

| VALUES | LEAD TO UNHELPFUL MESSAGES | WHICH RESULT IN THE DRIVERS |
|---|---|---|
| Achievement, autonomy, success, being right | Don't: make a mistake, take risks, be natural or childlike | Be perfect |
| Consideration, kindness, service | Don't: be assertive, important, different or say 'no' | Please |
| Speed, efficiency, responsiveness | Don't: take too long, relax or waste time | Hurry up |
| Courage, strength, reliability | Don't: show your feelings, give in or ask for help | Be strong |
| Persistence, patience, determination | Keep trying, don't be satisfied, don't relax | Try hard |

Remember that it's not the values themselves that cause our stress problems – it's when we let those values get out of perspective. For instance, if you're just about to leave work and notice that there are too many spaces in the heading on your report, and you have to run for the train because you couldn't leave until you'd edited it, your 'be perfect' driver is having a negative effect on your stress.

# HOW THE DRIVERS CAN AFFECT US

### 'BE PERFECT' BECKY

She speaks in completed sentences, often numbering off various points. Her clothes are very co-ordinated and elegant. She is known for her high standards. She is good at focusing on the work in hand and always sees the best way of completing a task.

Becky gets stressed by anything she sees as other people's 'low' standards or illogicality. As her stress increases, she becomes more and more single-minded, seeing only her own point of view.

### 'PLEASE' PETE

Pete loves to spend time with other people and is usually the first to break the ice at a social gathering. He feels responsible for those around him and tries to be pleasant and helpful to everyone, often doing things for them without having to be asked.

Pete gets stressed when he's criticized, as he then feels as though everyone has misunderstood him. As his stress increases, Pete gets emotional and feels upset that people have ignored his hard work.

### 'HURRY UP' HARJINDER
Harjinder uses lots of phrases like: 'quick', 'get going', 'hurry up', 'don't waste time', 'there's no time to ...'. He often speaks rapidly, and will usually be doing more than one thing at a time, and all of them enthusiastically.

Harjinder gets stressed by silence and having too much time to think. He hates feeling he's got nothing to do. As his stress increases he becomes impatient and interrupts people and he'll arrive late for things as he tries to fit a couple of extra jobs in before he leaves.

### 'BE STRONG' SUZIE
Suzie is good at working on her own, calmly and steadily, reliable even when the pressure is on. Her voice and body language don't give much away about her feelings.

Suzie gets stressed when she has to ask for help to get something done, or when she thinks people might see her as weak or vulnerable. As her stress increases Suzy withdraws even further into herself and becomes less able to deal with changes to her routine.

### 'TRY HARD' TONY
Tony uses the word 'try' a lot: 'I'm happy to give it a try', 'Yes, I'll try and get it finished'. In fact he's often the first to volunteer for work and likes to get involved in lots of things.

Tony gets stressed when he thinks people will criticize him for not doing enough. As his stress increases he makes a lot of promises about tasks he's going to take on, but never seems to finish anything.

You may recognize a bit of yourself in Becky, Pete, Harjinder, Suzie or Tony. If you do, then go back to the questions you answered Yes or Sometimes to in the relevant sections of the stress driver questionnaire. For each one ask yourself:

**What would happen if I said 'No' to this question?**
**How would I feel if I said 'No' to this question?**
**What messages have I had in my life about this?**
**Are these messages really helpful to me now?**

# RELAX
## AND LET GO OF YOUR STRESS

All of these exercises and activities will help to release some of the tension we carry around with us when we're stressed. Aim to build in a few periods of stress-release every day. If you're saying to yourself, 'I haven't got time for that,' get out your 'to do' list now and add 'relaxation' to it. Like any other exercise, you'll need to practise to become good at relaxing. After a while, the exercises actually save you time as you will be more energetic and able to deal with whatever comes your way more effectively. You can do these whatever your state of physical fitness.

## BREATHING

As odd as it sounds, just concentrating on your breathing for a few moments will help to reduce the stressful chatter in your mind. By focusing on your own breathing pattern you're diverting a bit of brain capacity away from thinking about whatever is stressing you.

## TAKE A TEN-SECOND HOLIDAY

You can do this at any time and in any place. Get into the habit of having several of these during the day.

- **If you are sitting, put your feet flat on the floor and your hands loosely in your lap. If you are standing, place your feet comfortably apart and, if you can, let your arms hang by your sides.**
- **Breathe in slowly to the count of five. Make sure you fill your lungs and expand your abdomen as you breathe. Notice how your spine stretches slightly as you do this.**
- **Breathe out slowly to the count of five, keeping your spine slightly stretched.**
- **Bring your breathing back to normal and carry on with what you were doing.**

## THE FIVE-MINUTE REST CURE

Again, this is something you can do sitting at your desk or to help you sleep at the end of a busy day. You can even adapt it for when you are on a crowded bus.

Make sure you are as comfortable as possible if you are travelling. The main thing is to be balanced, so uncross your legs and arms, and give your back as much support as possible. It will work best if you can close your eyes.

- **Do three rounds of breathing as in the ten-second holiday.**
- **Notice the sounds of your body and tune out the sounds around you.**
- **Concentrate on each part of your body in turn, from head to toes. Imagine each part becoming warm and relaxed. Pay particular attention to your head, face, neck and hands.**
- **Keep your breathing slow and rhythmic as you move your attention through your body, matching the feeling of letting go to each out breath.**
- **When you've released the tension in your toes, take one more slow deep breath in and out.**
- **Open your eyes.**

If you can afford a bit of extra time for this exercise, try tensing up the various parts of your body, then relaxing them. This gives an even more relaxed feeling.

# MEDITATION

Here are some quick meditations (this may sound a bit of a contradiction, but they do work), which will help you to achieve a state of 'calm alertness', able to deal with stress without feeling harassed.

Before each one, use the ten-second holiday breathing technique and keep your breathing steady. Sit as comfortably as you can without slumping. The idea is to relax, without falling asleep.

Remember that you are in control – if you experience distracting or uncomfortable thoughts you can simply notice them and choose to come back to the relaxed state you are creating for yourself.

### Beautiful place

In your mind's eye create a place where you can feel happy and peaceful. It can be somewhere you have been and know, or somewhere specially created. Make the picture as full as you can – notice the sounds and smells as well as the sights. Imagine that you are looking around and see it from different angles. Make a special place for yourself in the picture – the most secluded seat or a particular tree to lean against, for example. Then you can return here whenever you like, knowing it is waiting for you.

### Sounds

Just let yourself actually hear every sound around you and within yourself. Separate out each one and notice their pitch, volume and quality.

### The body vase

Imagine yourself as a you-shaped glass vase. At the start you are full of a cloudy, rather murky liquid. Imagine that you have taps on the ends of your fingers and toes and when you open them the liquid level slowly goes down as all the stress runs out of your body. When it's all gone, close the taps.

Now picture a hole in the top of your head. A clear, sparkling, refreshing liquid is pouring in, filling you with calmness and strength. When your whole vase is full, close the hole. You are now ready to open your eyes and carry on with your life with renewed vigour.

# PHYSICAL EXERCISE

For a while now we've known about the dangers of deep-vein thrombosis (DVT) for long-haul air passengers. Some doctors are now saying that those of us who sit at any activity for lengthy periods need to take regular physical breaks, so here are some suggestions.

### Screensaver

If you spend a long time working at a computer screen you'll know how tired and achy you become. Take a short break every hour or so to move or turn away.

- Close your eyes and relax your face. Keeping your fingers together gently massage your forehead and move your fingers in circles around your eyes. Repeat in one direction, then move the opposite way.
- Put your fingers on your forehead and gently rub your temples with your thumbs.
- Close your eyes and cup your hands over them. Hold for a count of 20.

### The neck and shoulder workout

- Put your hands over your shoulders. As you breathe out, let your head fall back and slowly bring your fingers over your collarbones.
- Place your left hand on your right shoulder and gently squeeze and release it. Repeat along the upper and lower arm. Then do the same for the other shoulder and arm.
- Put your hands lightly on the top of your head. Gently pull your head down and hold the position. Notice the slight stretch in the back of your neck.
- Raise one shoulder and gently rotate it backwards, then repeat with the other shoulder.

### The leg stretch

Keeping one foot flat on the floor, gently raise your other leg a few centimetres (a couple of inches) from the floor. Rotate your foot one way and then the other. Repeat with the other leg.

Get up from your seat and walk at least ten paces before sitting down again.

# 8 CREATIVITY AT WORK

*Once upon a time, creativity was assumed to be separate from every day life, best left to artists and poets, certainly nothing to do with the 'real world' of science or business, where 'wacky' ideas were not welcome. Creativity, like intuition and inspiration, was something indefinable, and probably you were either born with it or you weren't. Yet science needs – and indeed makes – intuitive leaps, and businesses need innovation or they'll stagnate and fail.*

## WHERE DOES IT COME FROM?

Is creativity, like spontaneity, something which just happens? If so, how will we know when it will happen? What many people do know is that being summoned to a meeting room so that 'We can all have fun and bounce ideas around' is almost guaranteed to stop their creative juices flowing.

Two French mathematicians, Poincarre and Hadamard, were the first to give the creative process a structure:

**Preparation**
You try to solve a problem using normal means.

▶ **Incubation**
You get frustrated when these methods don't work so you go off and do something else.

▶ **Illumination**
The answer appears in a flash.

▶ **Verification**
Reasoning takes over again as you assess whether or not the new idea is any good.

# CURRENT THINKING
# ABOUT THINKING

Until recently, people thought that there were two types of thinking that lead to creativity:

**'convergent thinking' – drawing on all your resources to solve a problem**
**'divergent thinking' – solving a problem by seeing it in a different way**

Some people appeared to be better at divergent thinking than others. Although we now know that it is a more complex issue, these two models are nevertheless helpful in looking at creative processes, as we'll see later.

## THE WIDER VIEW

Howard Gardner, who identified many of the different 'intelligences' (see page 18), suggests taking a wider view, saying that there are many different ways to be creative, including verbal, visuo-spatial, and so on. Other psychologists say it is simply a state of mind, a readiness and willingness to let creative ideas form.

Whatever view they take of it, most people now agree that we can *learn* to be more creative. Using the analogy of sport, some people undoubtedly are born with the potential to break the 100-metre sprint record, while the rest of us will never do it. But assuming basic good health, everyone can get a bit fitter, whether walking, running or in a wheelchair. So you may not be the person who comes up with the next 'big idea' but you can learn thinking techniques that will help you generate more ideas.

## *Businesses need creativity or they fail*

# IT'S A BRAINWAVE

Our brain transmits waves of electrical impulses at different speeds depending on what it's doing. Current research is looking at the 'state of flow' of these brain waves.

There are four states:
**Beta** is the fastest (about 13–25 cycles per second) and is how our brain is working for most of the time when we're awake.
**Alpha** (8–12 cycles per second) is the state our brain is in when it is having ideas.
**Theta** (4–7 cycles per second) is when we are in the first part of sleep.
**Delta** (half a cycle per second) is the state of our brain when deeply asleep.

Obviously, to do our best thinking we would like our brains to be in the **alpha** state. So how can we reach it? Some people seem to do it easily, even accidentally, while others need to work at it. Relaxation techniques have been shown to slow brain waves down to the alpha frequency. So, if you adopt some of the ways of dealing with stress from the last chapter, it seems that you *will* be able to have more creative ideas.

# LOOKING FOR ALTERNATIVE EXPLANATIONS

As we've seen, our minds are good at making connections – that's how they work, after all – but this is not necessarily helpful if you're trying to be creative. As the brain tries to connect a new thought with what's already known, patterns get set and it becomes harder to think differently. We've also become conditioned to the idea that there's always one 'right answer'. For example, participants on a training course may be asked to go off and do an exercise or other learning task and then to present their results. A very common question is 'Have we done this right?' when in fact there is no one, right, best way.

Sometimes, we are so keen to get an idea, any idea, that we settle too soon for one that presents itself, especially if it fits with what we are expecting. This is why we often get stuck with glib, over-generalizations. It's also why comedians use unexpected outcomes to their stories. The 'non-connectedness' jolts us out of our thinking pattern and raises a laugh.

Of course, time is important and we can't just go on and on thinking about an issue indefinitely – we have to call a halt at some point. But if we let ourselves carry on after the first 'OK' idea we might get to a much better one.

## What do you see?

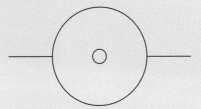

One way of answering this question might be: 'Some black lines on a blue page.' Let's change the question: **what might this be?**

List as many alternatives as you can. Some suggestions are on page 139.

Changing 'What do you see?' to 'What (or why) might this be?' can lead to some creative thinking in many situations.

For example, let's take the rather general statement 'The trouble with having school-leavers in the office is that they do only their set hours then leave on the dot of five.'

**What do you see?**
Some school-leavers going home at five o'clock.

**Why might this be?**
- They have no commitment to the company. (This is the point at which some people stop thinking.)
- They are keen on out-of-work activities.
- They want to get out of office clothes as quickly as possible.
- They don't know they are supposed to stay on after five.
- They don't like the office environment.
- They are studying after work.

This simple technique can generate lots of ideas. If you were responsible for the career development of young people in your organization, you could now look at ways to make sure they were fully aware of expectations, give them feedback about the impact of what they do, offer ways to make studying easier or find ways to make the environment attractive to them.

Try **'why might this be?'** questions on these scenarios. Keep going, even when you think you've got an 'obvious' answer.
- The car park is always full by the time I get here.
- The stationery cupboard is a mess.
- Fred is always late to meetings.

# WHERE TO USE
## CREATIVITY AT WORK

*You can use it anywhere and everywhere. You don't need to say, 'I think I'll be creative now,' or schedule it into your diary (although you can if you want). Just remember that you have a brain capable of creative thought at any time and let your mind be open to the possibilities.*

Here are some principles of creativity to bear in mind:

**Creativity is there already – let it happen**

**Aim for relaxed attention**

**Build up – don't knock down**

**Challenge the 'givens'**

**Manage the process – structure provides freedom**

## ACTIVITY

Try some of the techniques on the following pages and you'll soon find that you are able to apply your creativity in all sorts of situations. Some of the techniques you can simply do as you are; others may need a bit of space or other resources. Don't hold back from getting what you need, though – the increased creativity will be worth it.

## RANDOM WORD CONNECTIONS

**1 When you want more ideas use one of the following ways to get a random word.**

- Choose a book at random from the shelf. Open it anywhere. Close your eyes and put your finger on the page. Open your eyes and see what word you have chosen.
- Put a newspaper on the table in front of you. Choose a number between one and twenty. Open the paper at that page, count down that number of lines and then that number of words from the start of that line to choose a word.
- Close your eyes for a second and use the first thing or word you see in your mind's eye.

**2 Then think about all the ways your word is connected to the thing you are struggling with.**

For example, suppose you are responsible for organizing a seminar for senior staff from all your organization's branches. You are doing well with your 'to do' list, but you want to make sure you've covered everything. Get a random word (say, for instance that you opened a newspaper at a section on social services and got **'cares'**). How could this word help you generate more ideas?

**Cares: caring for delegates outside formal sessions**

> How can people contact me beforehand if they've got any concerns about timings, arrangements?

▶ What about anyone with special needs?

▶ Has the venue got accessible toilets?

If you get a word like 'it' or 'a', use the technique again to get a different word. Don't look down the page until you find a word you like, as this won't be random and may be too closely connected to your original thought process.

# METAPHOR

This can be a very powerful technique to help you look at a situation from a new angle. What you do is ask yourself, 'How is my situation like a ...?' You can look for metaphors in a variety of places.

Choose a setting from last night's TV programmes: **'How is my situation like a police station, a coffee bar or a doctor's waiting room?'**

Use the hobbies of people you know: **'How is my situation like knitting a jumper, cooking Chinese food or walking in the country?'**

Look at objects or situations outside the window: **'How is my situation like a tree, a traffic jam or a postal van?'**

**Note**: *You need only one metaphor each time – several are listed here to give you the idea.*

Then list as many similarities as you can between the thing you are thinking about and that metaphor. Next add the aspects of your situation that the list leads you to. But don't worry if you don't get any new ideas.

Here is an example of how you can apply a metaphor to a situation:

**How is organizing a conference like knitting a jumper?**
- Needs a pattern (programme; people need to know what's going on)
- Check size as going along (conference objectives clear?)
- Lots of skill involved (have I got all the skills? Where can I get help?)
- Wool gets tangled (hitches are only to be expected)
- Different pieces, come together only at end (obvious)
- Need to see if it fits (don't forget feedback forms for delegates)

This is also a great technique to use quietly to yourself when you want to be the person who adds something useful to a discussion. In your mind, come up with a metaphor for the subject at hand, and use it to generate a further discussion point or idea. If you're sitting in a meeting and the others keep going round and round in circles in their discussion about who should have which spaces in the car park. You *think* 'How is this like ... (take a quick look out of the window) a tree? Branches ▶ shelter for small birds ▶ shelter = security ▶ people leaving late at night worried about security.' ▶ You *say* 'How about we reserve the spaces near the building for people who work the late shift?'

## ACTIVITY

Now have a go yourself. List as many ways as possible that organizing a conference is like a doctor's waiting room.

Now choose your own metaphor and see if you can come up with even more ideas about organizing a conference.

### What would your mother think?

For this one you choose someone who you know a bit about (even if it's only what you've read about them in the papers). So it could be your mother, or a more famous person. Then you simply list all the things that this person might say and do if faced with your situation. Some of them might lead you to new, helpful ideas about your situation, others might not.

Back to that conference you're organizing.

### How would William Shakespeare handle it?
- He'd write a play: remember to get speaker's notes in time to prepare handouts.
- Theatre in the round ... make sure people at the back will be able to see and hear ... get a view screen and microphones?

# How is writing a report like baking a cake?

## Memory cards

These are something you can have a bit of fun with and keep adding to over a period of time.

- Get hold of a pack of small blank index cards.
- On each one, write and/or draw an object, an animal, an activity, a sport or a famous person. Add your own categories.
- Then when you're short of an idea for one of the activities above, you can use your cards to jog your thinking.

## REVERSE QUESTION

This can be helpful when you are generating solutions to a problem. Ask questions that reverse what you are trying to do such as: 'What would happen if we *didn't* do whatever it is?' Or 'What would it be like if we did the opposite thing to what we're talking about?' For example, you have a backlog of orders and are considering how to get staff to agree to work late, ask the reverse question:

How could we make staff leave early?

| ANSWERS TO REVERSE QUESTION | POSSIBLE NEW THOUGHTS |
| --- | --- |
| Make sure all work's finished before 5 | Maybe a shorter lunch? |
| Remove kettles and refreshment machines after 5 | Provide extra refreshments after 5 |
| Turn off the heating/air-conditioning | Make the environment more comfortable |

# ANTI-CREATIVITY – WHY WE DON'T LET CREATIVITY HAPPEN

You may have found, as you read the previous sections, that you were beginning to think of some of your own situations in new ways. But at the same time, a little voice in your head was whispering, 'It will never work,' 'They tried that last year,' or 'It's all very well for her, in her ivory tower.' The same thing happens when we hear other people's creative ideas.

It's as if the creative part of our brain is trying to get its own ideas heard (and other people's acknowledged) above a cacophony of moaners and whingers. Try to notice when this happens and challenge these 'voices' with a counterargument of your own.

Once you get the hang of challenging anti-creativity, you will get better at allowing creative ideas to flow, both yours and other people's. You will be contributing to a generally positive atmosphere in which creative thinking will flourish.

| INTERNAL MOAN | CHALLENGE |
| --- | --- |
| It's impractical. | Let's look for parts of it that will work. |
| It's too expensive. | Is there part of it we could do more cheaply? |
| I'll be laughed at. | Many great ideas started off by being ridiculed. |
| It's risky. | What's the worst that can happen? |
| I'll lose face if my junior staff has the 'winning' idea. | Haven't they done well under my management? It will reflect well on me. |
| I can't accept that this new person has had a better idea than me. | I'm glad I work in a place where we're not stuck in a rut. |
| This new idea might make my work up to now useless. | My work has been a good foundation, and this idea hasn't come from nowhere. |
| I don't want anyone else to get the credit. | I can also get credit for supporting good ideas and finding ways to implement them. |
| It's a good idea but no one 'upstairs' will listen. | Let's find appropriate ways to 'sell' our idea. |
| I don't like the person who's come up with this idea. | I may not like them but I can respect their intelligence. |

# INSTANT INSPIRATION

Try these if you need a quick boost to your creativity.

## 1 How many words?

Write the key word from your problem down and make as many words as you can using those letters. See what those new words help you to think of.

For example: CONFERENCE

**cone    core    once    free    fence    fern    concern    none**

Then pick up on any words that strike you:
**Fence: security arrangements**
**Free: goody bags for delegates**
**Once: repeat popular workshop sessions**

## 2 Draw a picture

It can be of the problem, or of your ideal solution, or of any stage in between. Now imagine you are an art expert explaining its meaning to someone who knows nothing about it. You may find new insights that you hadn't thought of before.

## 3 Soundtrack

What song or piece of music would be most appropriate as backing music for your problem? Why?

## 4 Back to school

Imagine you have to explain your idea to a class of bright eight-year-olds. What visual aids will you use? What sort of questions will they ask?

## 5 Hold the front page

Write a newspaper headline that sums up your idea. Use whatever style you like – getting it into tabloid format is challenging but fun.

# GENERATING IDEAS IN GROUPS

*When you are in a group all the same guidelines for creativity apply as when you are alone: the environment needs to be right and mental attitudes need to be positive. Bear in mind, however, that you also need to be aware of other issues such as group dynamics and power play between participants.*

**The five basic principles for group thinking:**

1 No criticism or judgment while ideas are flowing
2 Freewheeling – thinking in any direction is welcome
3 Quantity of ideas is more important than quality
4 All ideas must be recorded
5 A period of incubation should be allowed

## WHAT YOU NEED TO RUN A SUCCESSFUL GROUP-THINKING SESSION

### Someone to run it

Ideally, get someone who's not involved in the decision or problem. If that's really not feasible, choose someone who has some skills in chairing or facilitating. It's usually best *not* to choose the boss or the most senior person present, as this can make it hard for some people in a group to relax and feel free to express their ideas. Once you've chosen your facilitator, that person should stay in that role and not get involved in generating ideas.

### A clear purpose

Everyone present should know why they're there. It can be very helpful to spend a few minutes at the start going right round the group, hearing what everyone thinks the purpose is.

### A clear time frame

People will feel much more comfortable if they know what's going on. It's much better to have, say, an hour now and time to come back if we need it than to imply that everyone's got to sit here until this thing's sorted.

## A clear process

The facilitator gives everyone a rough outline of what will happen. (This can either have been agreed beforehand with the promoter of the project or is worked out on the day with the people involved.) It is also important to set out the five basic principles (see opposite).

## Procedures for running group sessions

1 Welcome everyone and make sure they're all comfortable.
2 Explain your role, the five basic principles and that all participants are equal partners in the process.
3 Explain what will happen and how long has been set aside.
4 Check that everyone understands the purpose of the meeting. Write it up on a flipchart sheet.
5 Try one of the following to get as many solutions up as possible:
 • Ask everyone to call ideas out. (You may need someone to help you write them up, alternately, on two flipcharts.) Make sure you write exactly what they say.
 • Put people in twos or threes to think of as many solutions as they can. They then come and write them on the flip sheets ranged around the room.
 • Ask people to write their ideas on sticky notes (one per note) and stick them to flip sheets ranged around the room. Everyone then walks round the room, seeing what new ideas are triggered by seeing the ones already written up.
 • If ideas start to dry up, try one of the creative techniques from earlier in the chapter (**metaphors**, **random words**, **instant inspirations**, and so on). It can be fun to use one of the creative techniques at the start, not just because ideas have dried up, but to get everyone thinking. It's important not to let this part run on and on; people will get fed up, especially if they think you (or someone else) is dragging it out until the right answer emerges.
6 Take a refreshment break.
7 Go back to the original problem and check that no one wants to rephrase it. (Sometimes one of the ideas that have been generated makes the problem look a bit different.)
8 Do one other technique to pull out any more ideas. By now people might be ready for something a bit different, so put them into small groups and give each group a blank sheet of flip sheets and lots of pens, and ask them to draw a picture of the problem as they see it being solved and the stages they will have gone through to get there.
9 Make sure all the ideas are visible to everyone. Give everyone a coloured pen and ask them to walk around the room and mark the ideas they like. They put three stars by their favourite, two stars by their second favourite and one by their third. Encourage them not to be swayed by where others are putting their stars.
10 Look at the ideas that have come out on top and write them on a new flipchart sheet.
11 This will probably be the final product of this session. You will need another session to look at ways to implement solutions.

# 9 COMMUNICATING YOUR IDEAS

*As well as processing all the information coming in, our brains prepare the messages that will go to the outside world to let other people know what we are thinking.*

## COMMUNICATIONS QUESTIONNAIRE

Read the statements and rate each one with the number that best describes your response:

0: Completely disagree
1: Disagree a bit more than agree
2: Agree a bit more than disagree
3: Completely agree

**1**  I have a wide vocabulary and I use it.
**2**  I can usually find more than one way to say the same thing.
**3**  I feel confident when I have to talk about my ideas.
**4**  People say that I am never lost for words.
**5**  I am aware of the particular 'jargon' of my own specialism, and those of other people I work with.
**6**  I have an interesting speaking voice.
**7**  I vary the speed at which I speak, depending on what I am talking about and how I feel about it.
**8**  I like the way I speak and I am proud of my accent, if I have one.
**9**  Other people do not have any trouble hearing me, even in a large group.
**10**  My tone of voice usually complements my actual words.
**11**  I feel comfortable about looking people in the eye when I am speaking.
**12**  I think gestures and other forms of body language communicate as much as words.
**13**  I think about what I will wear and how I look before a presentation.
**14**  I am aware of my own 'personal space', as well at that of other people.
**15**  I believe age, race, gender, size and other personal characteristics affect communication.
**16**  When I have to talk about something serious, I choose the best time and place to do it.
**17**  I wait until I think the other person is likely to be in a receptive mood.
**18**  When I have something to tell a colleague, I think about whether to send an email, make a phone call or speak face to face.
**19**  I use a range of visual aids if I am making a formal presentation.
**20**  If I need to be convincing, I spend as long thinking about the person I am dealing with as I do in preparing what I am going to say.

Now add up your scores.

# WHAT YOUR SCORE MEANS

**41 and above**   You think about what will help to make your communication a **success**. You are prepared to put some effort into it as you are aware that there's more to the message than mere words. You make a conscious effort to make sure that your words are backed up by your body language and tone of voice. People will find you believable and easy to understand.

**Between 21 and 40**   When your message is fairly straightforward you will be **heard** and **understood**. You spend time thinking about what you'll say so you may sometimes be surprised if people don't get the message straight away. You are aware that you may be giving unclear signals with your body language so you may try to minimize it by choosing your words even more carefully.

**Below 20**   You feel a bit lacking in **confidence** when it comes to **expressing** yourself. People sometimes fail to grasp your point, or seem to misunderstand you, and this may add to your frustration. You're not always sure when to speak up, so sometimes you miss an opportunity to get heard. You think that if only people would listen properly to what you're saying, you are actually quite clear.

## Following up

The questionnaire does, in fact, look at four vital areas of communication. Look at your score in each section to see where you are strongest. We then explore each in turn over the next few pages.

**Questions 1–5**   **Verbal Communication:** Score .................

**Questions 6–10**   **Vocal Communication:** Score .................

**Questions 11–15**   **Visual Communication:** Score .................

**Questions 16–20**   **Preparation:** Score .................

# TYPES OF
# COMMUNICATION

## VERBAL COMMUNICATION

Many of us are conscious that we have slightly different vocabularies for different parts of our lives. We probably learned as teenagers that some of the words we used with our peers were not acceptable at home, and vice versa. At work you may speak differently in a formal situation than when you are in the coffee lounge. This is quite normal. The trick is to make sure that the words you use are appropriate to the message, the situation and the other person. For example, if you wanted to apologize for forgetting to post a letter you would not start off with, 'I regret to inform you ...', but, 'I'm sorry ...'.

## VOCAL COMMUNICATION

Research has shown that when we first speak to someone, only 7 per cent of the first impression we create comes from the actual words we use, while 38 per cent comes from the way that we speak. As we get to know the other person and understand more about them these percentages change slightly, but it is still true that all the time we are communicating, the words are the least significant part. Another name for vocal communication is 'paralanguage'. It's all the aspects of language that are to do with the voice rather than the words.

| | | | |
|---|---|---|---|
| **tone** | **pitch** | **fluency** | **volume** |
| **speed** | **pauses** | **accent** | |

We often express our feelings through paralanguage. If a colleague says, 'No, I'm fine, don't worry about me,' with a sigh and a downward inflection of their voice, we can guess that they are not 'fine' at all, especially if there are visual clues as well, like a shrug or averted eyes.

A certain tone, just attached to one word or phrase, can alter the whole meaning of a message. For example:
**'This exciting opportunity ...' (said with a sneer)**
**'I love this job.' (said with a humourless laugh)**

### Controlling vocal communication

You *can* have control over all aspects of paralanguage, even your accent. The trick is awareness of **how your voice sounds** and **the impact on others**.

For example, try to notice what happens to your voice when you're angry, excited or nervous. When you are talking to someone and you are aware that you feel one of these things, it can be very helpful (to both of you) to name the feeling. **So: 'I'm a bit nervous about saying this ...' will help your listener to put your message into context and help you to control your nerves.**

Once you have begun to notice what your voice does, give yourself an internal cue to change it, set in positive terms. For example, your inner voice saying, 'Keep your volume up,' will be more helpful than, 'Don't mumble.'

As for your accent – keep it. It is part of the real you. Certainly don't apologize for it, or try to remove it. If you notice particular words, phrases or intonations tend to get misheard or misunderstood, think about ways you could vary them. And check that it is your accent that's the real issue – could it be your choice of words? When speaking to multi-cultural audiences, it becomes obvious that phrases that 'everybody' knows just don't translate.

# VISUAL COMMUNICATION

This is sometimes called 'body language' but it's more than that. It is all the ways that we communicate without words. It can account for about 55 per cent of a first impression, and around 50 per cent of any communication after that.

Types of visual communication include:
**facial expression**
**eye contact**
**physical proximity and contact**
**gestures**
**posture**
**appearance**

The main thing to remember about all types of visual communication is that they tend to be more easily believed than the verbal part. So if the visual communication matches the words, it will reinforce the message. But if it contradicts the words, it will be taken as the true meaning of the message.

All the things that you carry and wear give messages, too. We might wish they didn't, but it is worth giving some thought to what your appearance says and whether it is helping or hindering your communication.

# PREPARING TO
## COMMUNICATE

*'When I am getting ready to reason with a person, I spend one third of my time thinking about myself and what I am going to say – and two thirds about the other person and what they are going to say.' Abraham Lincoln*

You want to talk to someone (your partner, a colleague) about something that's been bothering you. To avoid a shouting match, you prepare what you want to say, and in fact you mentally devise a whole 'script'. 'I'll say this, then they'll say that, then I'll say...', and so on. The trouble is, when you actually talk to the person, the script doesn't work out the way you'd planned. This is partly because the other person didn't get a copy of the script beforehand, and partly because you spent too long thinking about your viewpoint and not enough about theirs.

A similar thing happens in all sorts of situations:

**In a seminar when the presenter uses too many slides because they've got a lot of information to impart. They haven't given a thought to the audience, some of whom know most of it already and all of whom have just had a good lunch.**

**When a manager who's heard that walking around to chat to staff is a good thing perches on your desk to tell you about a new directive from head office, totally disregarding the fact that you are obviously reading a lengthy document.**

In each case, the message is good, important and interesting, and the person delivering it is pleasant, enthusiastic and good at their job. But unless they work harder at looking from the other person's point of view, they will have wasted their breath.

## *Real conversations don't follow a script*

# THE VIEW FROM YOUR HILLTOP

When you talk to someone else about a topic, it's fairly obvious that they will see it from a different viewpoint to you. It may be completely different or only slightly, but they are not you, so it will be different.

The understanding gap is made wider because each of us is standing on a virtual hilltop made up of our own experience and background, feelings, values and beliefs.

If we want someone to be persuaded about our view we have two options:
- **climb their hill**
- **get them to climb ours**

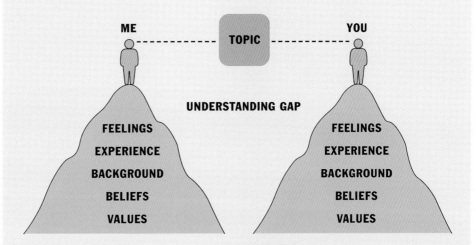

Climbing their hill will involve you asking questions like:
**What experience have you had of this?**
**What do you feel about this?**
**What do you believe is the right way to do this?**

Getting them up your hill will involve you telling them:
**Your experience**
**How you feel**
**Your beliefs about it**

The most persuasive communicators will do a bit of both, remembering that their own view at any stage may be different to the other person's.

# GETTING YOUR IDEAS ACROSS
# AT MEETINGS

*It doesn't matter how brilliant your idea is, if you don't pitch it correctly and don't communicate it effectively, it's not going to happen. Careful preparation beforehand and how you behave and speak during the meeting will at least help to ensure that your thoughts get a fair hearing.*

### Before the meeting

1 Make sure you have everything you need, relevant papers and so on.
2 Think about who'll be there: which people will be your allies and which will disagree.
3 If at all possible, talk to the other people beforehand to canvass their views, check what they are going to say and share information.
4 Think about where you'll sit. Get there early and choose a good place where everyone will be able to see you. In a formal meeting it's good to sit near the person chairing it, so that you are central and visible. If you are allocated a place that's inconvenient or uncomfortable, ask to move, or at least get the source of discomfort removed. For example, it will be difficult to speak well if you have bright sunlight shining straight into your eyes.

### At the meeting

1 Speak up early in the meeting with a positive comment. For example, when the chair asks for views, even if it's not particularly important that you contribute to this particular point say, 'I agree with all that's been said so far.' This gets your voice out into the air, and avoids it squeaking when your real turn comes, and people will have a positive 'vibe' about you.
2 Sometimes you need to use a physical signal that you want to contribute to a discussion – change your posture by leaning forward or briefly hold up your hand.
3 Take a breath before you speak.
4 Introduce yourself if some people don't know who you are, or you missed earlier introductions (not all chairs are good at remembering introductions).
5 Start on a positive note. For example: 'Derek's idea is interesting, although I disagree about the costings,' is more positive than starting with, 'I disagree...'. Make sure your positive note is actually true though, otherwise you'll sound insincere. Avoid clichés like the plague! Most people mistrust, 'with respect' and interpret it as, 'I have no respect for you, you fool.'
6 Remember to check that your verbal, vocal and visual messages all match up.

**7** Keep your eye contact appropriate and include everyone as you look around. Remember not to assume too much from people's facial expressions. Don't be put off by the person scowling – they may just be concentrating – and don't be tempted to favour the person smiling – they may be daydreaming.

**8** If you have a lot to say, break it up into manageable chunks and summarize as you go along. If you are making a recommendation or a proposal make it clear what you are asking the people at the meeting to do and help the person making the notes by letting them know what you want recorded.

### Other useful interventions in meetings

If you don't understand something – ask. The chances are that you'll be thanked afterwards by others who didn't understand either but were too afraid to ask.

If you notice the discussion is going off the point or going over the same thing again and again, it's not undermining the chair to say, 'I propose we move on.' Then it's open to anyone else to make a counterproposal. But it's much more likely most of them will agree with you.

# EXERCISES TO BUILD UP YOUR COMMUNICATION SKILLS

### Verbal

**1** Find a clearer way to say each of the following:
   **a) It would be much appreciated if you'd let me have your response by Friday.**
   **b) We are in an ongoing staff shortage situation.**
   **c) This activity will not be able to be implemented for some considerable time.**
   **d) An adequate explanation for the delay was not forthcoming from the suppliers.**
   **e) Alternative strategies for the realization of our objectives will have to be determined.**

**2** Which is the correct word to use in these sentences?
   **a) A referee should be .......................... in the match result.**
   *disinterested or uninterested*
   **b) This checkout is for six items or ..............................**
   *fewer or less*
   **c) Our new boss was .................................... in the pub trade.**
   *formally or formerly*
   **d) How will the changes ...................... you?**
   *effect or affect*
   **e) We have changed our ............................ supplier.**
   *stationery or stationary*

**3** Find a positive way of expressing each of the following ideas:
   **a) Three out of ten people can't operate the new system.**
   **b) I disagree with most of what Sue says.**
   **c) I'm hopeless at estimating how much paper we'll need.**
   **d) It's no good talking to George when he's in a mood.**
   **e) Everyone knows that's a stupid idea.**

## Vocal

**1** See how changing the tone of your voice affects sound and meaning.
   **a) Read the following sentence out loud eight times, putting the emphasis on a different word each time. Notice the effects on the sound and meaning of the sentence.**
   *The office has been painted green and white.*
   **b) Now think of a feeling (anger, joy, sorrow or fear) and read the sentence aloud with that feeling in mind. How is the sound affected?**
   **c) Now read the sentence aloud in a monotone. Think about how this would sound to a listener.**

**2** Read each of the following sentences aloud a) as if it's a question, b) as if it's bad news, and c) as if it's an exciting discovery.
   **The photocopier has broken down again.**
   **Tom wants a cheese sandwich for lunch.**
   **We've just recruited an excellent new accountant.**
   Notice what happens to your tone, pitch, speed and volume in each case.

## Visual

**1** Stand in front of a mirror. Say each of the following sentences aloud, trying to match appropriate gestures and facial expressions to the words.
   **a) I'm really pleased to meet you.**
   **b) This is a huge problem.**
   **c) I'm annoyed that you've arrived late again.**
   **d) I'm rather embarrassed about mentioning your poor spelling.**
   **e) It's my fault, I'm sorry.**
   Now say them again, this time trying to use gestures and facial expressions which will convey an opposite (or at least different) message to the words. Notice which you found easiest and hardest to do. Which feelings are you most comfortable expressing?

**2** Observation: next time you have the chance, turn on a TV discussion programme and turn the sound down. Watch one participant's gestures, posture and facial expressions. What clues might these give you about the person and what they are saying? (Of course, you'll be able to check this only if you record the programme to compare later. But it is still an interesting exercise to see just how much you can pick up without words.)

**3** Next time you are in a public place with strangers try to tune in and listen to your inner voice and what it's telling you about the people you see.

What do you notice first about people, in the first split second? What does their age, race, size and gender make you think about them? This isn't about stereotyping – rather it's about noticing that we do make these snap decisions and allowing ourselves to challenge them.

## Non-verbal communication checklist:

### POSTURE AND DISTANCE
- Do you sit or stand upright or slouched?
- Are you too near to or too far from the other person?
- Are you higher or lower?

### EYES
- Is your gaze relaxed and friendly?
- Do you maintain appropriate eye contact?
- What is your expression when people approach you?

### MOUTH
- Do you clench your jaw?
- Is your smile genuine – or misleading?

### VOICE
- Note your tone, inflection and volume.
- Do you whine, or bellow?
- Does your tone convey sarcasm?
- Do you mumble or swallow your words?
- Be aware of the effects of your accent, if any.

### GESTURES
- What do you do when someone is approaching?
- Hand movements can be very expressive, but are they appropriate?
- Are your hands covering your mouth or fiddling with your hair, or clasped behind your back?
- Do you shift from one foot to the other?

### APPEARANCE
- What does your appearance say about you?
- Does it convey the impression that you want?

### BREATHING
- Noticing your breathing and learning to relax your body allows you to manage your feelings and communicate clearly.

# CONCLUSION

*This book has tried to give you some insights into how your brain works, when it is at its best – and when it's not working so well.*

- You've identified your strengths and weaknesses, some of which you probably already knew, and some which may have surprised you.
- You have tried some techniques which have already begun to develop your brain's amazing potential.

No one suddenly becomes a great thinker simply by reading a book, no matter how good it is. **Practising** and **implementing** new ideas will mean changing the way you see things and maybe taking a few risks.

Clearly, a major factor in whether you continue to keep up the good work you've already started and make even more progress, is the extent to which you are prepared to put it all into practice. Keeping your brain fit needs a deal of **commitment** and a regular analysis of your performance.

## CONTINUING SELF-ASSESSMENT

### Make a learning diary

A learning diary is a great resource for recording your development. You can track your progress and reflect on the benefits that it is having for you and your work.

### Reviewing what you've learned

Your first task is to look back over the chapters of this book and any notes you've made, and identify what you've learned or had confirmed about yourself so far. Then add a note about how this will be useful to you. Just aim for two or three key points in each section that strike you as you review.

# REVIEW TABLE

| TOPIC | WHAT I LEARNED OR HAD CONFIRMED | HOW I CAN USE THIS |
|---|---|---|
| **How well do I use my senses?** *(see pages 16–17)* | | |
| **How intelligent am I?** *(see page 18)* | | |
| **What kind of thinker am I?** *(see pages 25–8)* | | |
| **What's my learning style?** *(see page 30)* | | |
| **What's my personality type?** *(see page 33)* | | |
| **What competences do I have?** *(see pages 38–40)* | | |
| **How do I use my time?** *(see page 47)* | | |
| **What thinking blocks do I have?** *(see pages 52–3)* | | |
| **How do I solve problems?** *(see pages 54–7)* | | |
| **Do I operate in a 'thinking environment'?** *(see page 63)* | | |
| **How motivated am I?** *(see page 67)* | | |
| **Do I have CRISP objectives?** *(see pages 66–7)* | | |
| **How well do I understand my short-term memory?** *(see pages 72–4)* | | |
| **What techniques can I now use to improve my long-term memory?** *(see pages 78–82)* | | |
| **What are my stress drivers?** *(see pages 89–90)* | | |
| **How do I relax during my time at work?** *(see pages 93–5)* | | |
| **What techniques can I use to boost my creativity?** *(see pages 100–105)* | | |
| **How good are my communication skills?** *(see pages 108–9)* | | |
| verbal? | | |
| vocal? | | |
| visual? | | |

# DEVELOPMENT PLAN

Now you need to make a plan to develop yourself. Remember, development isn't only about overcoming your weaknesses – it can also be about enhancing your strengths.

Look again through the list you've made. Choose a few areas that you particularly want to work on. Don't be too ambitious – three would be a realistic number of things to focus on the first time round.

For each one, answer these questions:

**What words or phrases describe how, ideally, you'd like to be?**
For example, 'I want to be the one who comes up with ideas in meetings.'

**What four things will you have to do to achieve this?**
a) Ask questions to make sure I'm clear what we're talking about.
b) Put aside my fear of looking silly.
c) Listen fully to be able to build on others' ideas.
d) Try some instant creativity techniques.

**Where or when do you find it difficult to do this at present?**
When Jane is chairing the meeting, because she often seems to have her own ideas and not listen to anyone else.

**What can you do to overcome this difficulty?**
Talk to Jane about some group idea generation techniques.

**Who or what can help you?**
I know Bill is also keen to have more creative meetings, he'll be an ally.

**When will you try it?**
I'll talk to Jane tomorrow, and then come up with some ideas at our strategy meeting on Tuesday.

If you are serious about development, it is worth writing your thoughts down. As you progress, you can look back over your notes and notice that things you once thought challenging are now becoming easier.

Put reviewing your learning diary on to your list of regular things to do. It will also be interesting to re-do some of the exercises and questionnaires in the book to see how you change as a result of putting the techniques into practice.

# YOUR DAILY BRAIN
# WORKOUT PLAN

**Every day**
Choose one activity in each category. Where appropriate, the answers are on page 140.

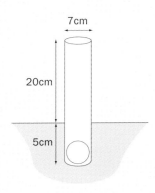

## Creativity and lateral thinking

◄ **1** How many ways can you think of to get the ball out, without damaging the ball, the tube or the floor?

**2** Who would you choose to play you in a film of your life? Why?

**3** If your organization was an animal, what would it be? Why?

**4** What comes next in this sequence?

**L  15  30  40  A  ?  ?  ?**

◄ **5** What could this be?

**6** What would be the theme song for the TV series about your life?

**7** Which is the odd one out? Why?

**17  3  2  7  12  11**

**8** Think of as many ways as possible to reframe this problem: Everyone needs more time off work.

◄ **9** Complete this drawing in whatever way you choose.

**10** Treat yourself to an intricate colouring book and some coloured pencils and spend half an hour colouring in.

# Analytical and logical thinking

**1** Fill in the missing number.

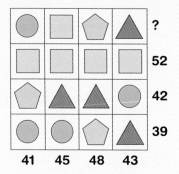

**2** Find the missing word.

123 = RAG
456 = NET
726 = SAT
7612435 = ?

**3** Fill in the missing squares.

| | | | |
|---|---|---|---|
| Zw6 | Xy5 | Yx3 | Wz4 |
| Wz5 | Yx3 | Xw4 | Zy6 |
| Yx3 | Wz4 | Zy6 | Xw5 |
| Xy4 | Zw6 | | |

**4** Which shape?

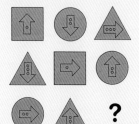

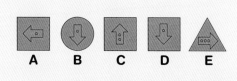

A    B    C    D    E

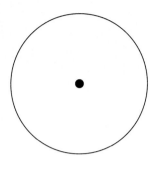

**5** Which of the following is not illustrated by this drawing?

| | |
|---|---|
| **End of a pencil** | **Cone** |
| **Wheel and axle** | **Wine glass** |
| **Long tube** | **Drawing pin** |
| **Salt cellar** | **Toffee apple** |
| **Spinning top** | **Circle with a dot in the middle** |

**6** Convert this to numbers.

```
  K J H
  N M P
H I Q Q
```

**7** How many ways are there to get from A to B by following the direction of the arrows?

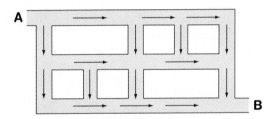

**8** I wrote four consecutive single numbers on four pieces of paper. Then I turned the papers over and wrote four consecutive single numbers on the back. On each piece of paper the two sides totalled 14. If my first four numbers add up to 30 and my second four add up to 26, what are the two numbers on each piece of paper?

**9** Which piece fits the square so that all rows and columns add up to the same total?

| 4 | | | 1 |
|---|---|---|---|
| 5 | | 2 | 5 |
| 2 | 6 | 2 | 3 |
| 2 | 4 | 3 | 4 |

A

| 1 | |
|---|---|
| 2 | 4 |

B

| 3 | 2 |
|---|---|
| 1 | |

C

| | 6 |
|---|---|
| 4 | 2 |

D

| 2 | 6 |
|---|---|
| 1 | |

E

| 3 | 4 |
|---|---|
| 4 | |

**10** Treat yourself to a logic puzzle magazine and try to solve one.

# Sense boosters

| SIGHT | Look at an object and focus on the spaces and shadows around it. | Look at a colour picture in a newspaper or magazine. Focus on the colours rather than the subject of the picture and notice all the shades and patterns. |
|---|---|---|
| HEARING | Listen to some music of a type you don't normally listen to. | Close your eyes and listen to the sounds around you. Try to picture how far away each of the objects or people is from you. |
| TOUCH | Close your eyes, reach out and touch your desk lightly with the tips of your fingers and gently move them over various objects. Try to visualize what your fingers are telling you. | One by one, name all the things that are touching you at this moment. |
| TASTE | Look at a picture in a cookery book or magazine. Imagine the tastes of the different foods and where you would feel them on your tongue. | One by one, touch the tip of your thumb to each of your finger tips in turn. Notice how different each one feels. |
| SMELL | Close your eyes and try to notice all the smells around you. They may be faint, and you will have to concentrate. | Look at a picture in a cookery book or magazine. Imagine the smells of the different foods. |

# Memory builders

**1**  Look at these items for two minutes.
Then cover them up and list or draw as many as you can.

**2**  Use your 'pegwords' or your 'walk around the house' to remember this list:

**ball**
**cards**
**train**
**marbles**
**puzzle**
**skates**
**bricks**
**doll**
**chess**
**book**

Cover it up and write it out from memory.

**3**  Study these for two minutes and cover them up. Draw as many as you can recall.

**4**   List as many as you can of the people you spoke to yesterday.

**5**   Use one of your memory tricks to learn this list:

**Santiago**
**Oslo**
**Warsaw**
**Rome**
**Washington**
**Pretoria**
**Wellington**
**Bangkok**
**Athens**
**Moscow**

Cover it up and write it out from memory.

**6**   Look at your desk for 2 minutes. List everything that is on it from memory.

**7**   Draw a sketch map of a route you are familiar with. Compare it to a map of the area.

**8**   Use one of your memory tricks to learn this list:

**Shoe**
**Jacket**
**Blouse**
**Sock**
**Dress**
**Coat**
**Tie**
**Scarf**
**Skirt**
**Sweater**

Cover the list up and write it out from memory.

**9** Study these items for 2 minutes. Cover them up and list or draw them from memory.

**10** Write the story of your first hour at work today.

# Polish up your linguistic intelligence

**1**   Complete the dishes:

_AS_ _ NE          GO_ _A_ _          _O _S_ A _A

_ A _ _ L _          _ U _ _ Y          H_ _ _U _ _ _ R

_ M _LE _ _ E          R _ _ I _L _          _ N _ H _ _A_ _S

**2**   Fill in this minimalist crossword.

**Across**                    **Down**
1. To surpass                 1. More than
3. Written composition    2. American city

|   | 1 | 2 |
|---|---|---|
| 3 |   |   |

**3**   What are:

**a) Hyssop      b) A teal      c) Teak      d) A borzoi   e) Gouda
f) An omnivore  g) Lapis lazuli  h) A plectrum  i) Pimento**

**4**   Change HEAD to TAIL, altering one letter at a time.

**HEAD**

_ _ _ _

_ _ _ _

_ _ _ _

_ _ _ _

**TAIL**

**5**   Each pair of words has answers that rhyme.

**a) GAME BIRD            PEN REFILL
b) HUMAN                ENTRANCE
c) YEARN FOR            DIG FOR
d) UNIT OF TIME         SONG BIRD
e) CULTIVATED AREA      SET LIKE CONCRETE
f) IMPOSING             BRIDGED**

**6** Add a different three-letter word to each list to make whole words.

**a)**
**ST** _ _ _
**BR** _ _ _
**L** _ _ _
**M** _ _ _
**W** _ _ _
**TH** _ _ _

**b)**
**ST** _ _ _
**BER** _ _ _
**L** _ _ _
**M** _ _ _
**CR** _ _ _
**DON** _ _ _

**c)**
**ST** _ _ _
**BR** _ _ _
**L** _ _ _
**H** _ _ _
**W** _ _ _
**BL** _ _ _

**7** What are the plurals of these words?

**Potato**
**Hoof**
**Reef**
**Deer**
**Ally**
**Alley**
**Journey**
**Child**
**Ox**
**Dance**
**Princess**
**Audience**

**8** The answers to these pairs of words are pairs that sound alike but are spelled differently. For example, FRUIT and TWO = PEAR and PAIR.

**CARRY and NAKED**
**CREATED and FEMALE SERVANT**
**KNOTTED and EBB AND FLOW**
**HELP and ASSISTANT**
**LEND and SOLO**
**HOUR and HERB**
**SHEEP and TREE**
**NUMBER and CONSUMED**
**VERSE and FROST**
**DISCOVER and MADE TO PAY**

**9** Anagrams: all of these words can have their letters rearranged to make another real word.

**THOUSAND**
**FIGHTER**
**LOVELY**
**INCLUDES**
**SUNLIGHT**
**TRANSIENCE**
**EDUCATION**
**PIECRUST**
**EARRING**
**HAPPIEST**
**INTRODUCE**
**DISPROVE**

**10** Synonyms: write a word in the brackets that means the same as the ones outside them.

**CONTAINER (          ) FIGHT**
**BIRD (          ) NO SCORE**
**CARRY (          ) ANIMAL**
**CORRECT (          ) A HAND**
**TREE (          ) YEARN**
**LEVEL (          ) STAGE SCENERY**
**HEARTH (          ) IRRITATE**
**SHIP'S SPEED (          ) TIED ROPE**

# Tone up your mathematical intelligence

**1** Thrifty Mrs Jones runs a hotel. She keeps all the little bits of soap the guests leave behind and she can make a new bar from every nine bits. How many new bars of soap can she make from 729?

**2** What's the missing number?

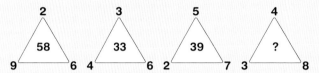

**3** If 1000 books cost $68.90 how much would 340 cost?

**4** Which is the odd one out?

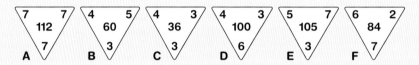

**5** When full, a barrel holds 75 litres of oil. How many litres are left when 40 per cent has been used?

**6** What is the missing number?

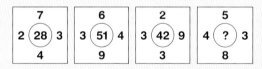

**7** The cake machine ices five cakes every minute. How many cakes will be iced in 8 hours if the machine keeps working at the same rate?

**8** A storage area measures 9m x 6m x 8m. How many boxes measuring 4m x 3m x 2m could you pack into it, assuming you had free access?

**9** Which is larger – 25 per cent of 180 or one-third of 138?

**10** Complete these sequences:

| 5 | 6 | 8 | 12 | 20 | ? | | |
|---|---|---|----|----|---|---|---|
| 2 | 4 | 3 | 9 | 4 | 16 | ? | ? |
| 81 | 72 | 64 | 57 | 51 | ? | | |

# Sharpen your other intelligences

Notice that all the things you do every day are using your wide range of intelligences. Remind yourself which ones you are using at any one time.

Be on the look-out for opportunities to develop the ones that you're less comfortable with:

**Visual**
Imagine you are *in* a picture in the newspaper. What would you see from behind the subject? From above? From below?

**Physical**
Notice the space that you are occupying. Imagine an artist is going to make a sculpture of you and has filled the space between you and the walls with a moulding material. What does your statue look like?

**Musical**
Imagine you are in an opera. If you can be private, sing a few lines to describe to the audience what is going on. What instruments would best accompany this scene?

**Social**
Look through your diary and contact list. Ring someone you haven't spoken to recently.

**Environmental**
Imagine you ran your organization. What measures would you introduce tomorrow to improve the working environment for your colleagues? What could you do in real life to achieve some of those improvements?

**Practical**
Find something to take apart and put back together again, even if it is only your pen. Study its component parts as you do it, and try to get an understanding of how they work.

**Emotional**
Draw a picture of a thermometer or other simple gauge. Plot your emotional state on it for a working day.

**Spiritual**
In whatever way feels right for you, let your mind rest on a big issue that you feel is important in the world. If appropriate, find someone you feel comfortable with and talk about this issue.

# BALANCING YOUR LIFE FOR A FITTER, HEALTHIER BRAIN

The phrase 'work–life balance' was almost unheard of ten years ago. We have moved on from the concept of 'juggling' career and family to 'balancing', which in theory sounds slightly more restful. In practice of course, many people are still struggling to deal with all the demands on their time, and in some organizations, flexible working is still equated with lack of commitment.

Some of the benefits of technology have also given rise to changes in work patterns and customer expectations that throw the concept of work–life balance into disarray:

- The speed of communication means that we are getting used to instant responses. We complain if we have to wait for supplies or services, and this puts stress onto those who provide them.
- Mobile phones mean that we need never be out of reach.
- Emails give a sense of urgency to messages that once would have waited in an in-tray without the organization grinding to a halt.

For many people, the boundary between home and work life is no longer clear, as more people use technology to work from home for some, if not all, of the working week. This may save on the stress of daily commuting, but adds pressure as people take on extra work to fill that 'extra' time and work harder to convince the organization that they are actually working.

Most of us are well aware what is happening to us. The old saying goes, 'No one lies on their death-bed and says, "I wish I'd spent more time at work,"' and have you heard the one about the graveyard being full of 'indispensable' people? Even if they are rather morbid, these comments show that we do see the connection between overwork and ill health, at the least.

Here are some questions to ask yourself:
**Do I work longer hours than I used to?**
**Do I work longer hours than I need to?**
**Am I achieving something important when I stay late at work, or am I just keeping busy?**
**Do I feel guilty if I leave the office before anyone else, or arrive later?**

# ACTIVITY

Try this exercise to identify what you could do about getting your life more in balance. In the first circle, draw segments that roughly represent the amount of time you give to each area of your life. It's not a scientific survey, you don't need to work out hours and minutes, simply get a general idea.

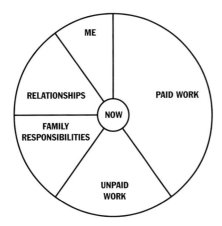

Then, in the second circle, draw the segments as you'd like them to be. Don't be constrained by reality – go for what you want.

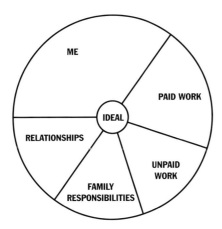

Which area has increased?

Which has decreased?

What would have to happen in real life for this change to take place?

# HEALTHY LIVING

*You probably know about the benefits of a healthy diet and regular exercise. You may even put the principles into practice. Just in case you don't, here are some pointers.*

## DRINKING

Drink plenty of water every day, at least two litres (4½ US pints). Most people live in a permanent state of partial dehydration, which means that their brains function at less than full capacity and their bodies take longer to dispose of waste products. Recent studies have shown that children who drink eight glasses of water a day do best in test results.

### Alcohol

Although there is a lot of water in beer, this isn't a reason to drink lots of it, or any other alcoholic drink. For some of us, alcohol causes us to be less inhibited and so may improve our creativity, but as alcohol is a depressant it also reduces the flow of blood to the brain and so reduces thinking power.

### Caffeine

Caffeine is a stimulant and has the effect of increasing alertness in the short term, but, as it is a diuretic, it also leads to dehydration. You should drink two glasses of water for every cup of coffee.

## *Most people live in a permanent state of partial dehydration*

# Healthy body, healthy mind

## EATING

We need a balanced diet. Our mothers told us this, and the only thing that has changed over the years is that experts now have a different idea about what constitutes a balanced diet. Diet is another area where innovation has not always led to improvement. Quick, convenient foods need a lot of pre-processing before they reach us, which in turn often means using additives and extra sugar and salt.

### What your body needs

Proteins break down to create chemicals which act as neurotransmitters. Simple carbohydrates like sugar give a quick burst of energy, and fats are needed to keep neural networks healthy and so are good for your memory. Salts are essential for all human cells to function, but need to be the right balance of sodium and potassium.

Fibre, vitamins and trace elements all play essential roles in keeping us healthy.

### Grazing

It all adds up to making sure you eat a range of foods every day. The traditional Western approach of three meals a day is giving way to a 'little and often' approach. 'Grazing' allows the whole body to receive a steadier supply of oxygenated blood and so the brain maintains a more constant state of alertness.

A big meal makes us feel sleepy because our digestive system takes more blood to enable it to function and so our brain doesn't get enough until the meal is digested. As long as you graze mainly on healthier, unprocessed foods, and drink plenty of water you will maintain energy and performance throughout the day.

# SLEEPING

As adults we need an average of eight hours sleep a night. Over time, lack of sleep can lead to poor concentration, low energy and mood swings or even mental ill health. Without enough sleep our brains do not function at their full capacity.

### Quality not quantity

Most people seem to need less sleep as they get older, but many of us impose sleep deprivation on ourselves long before we age by working too late, eating badly late in the day and not exercising. And it is not just the amount of sleep that counts – the *quality* is important too.

Your brain needs time to process all that has happened during the day, and it does this during periods of deep sleep, or REM (Rapid Eye Movement). The particular neurotransmitter which is produced during REM helps keep neural networks healthy and so improves the memory-forming process. So when we say we'll 'sleep on it' we actually do – the brain lays down memory traces while we sleep so that when we wake, it becomes easier to solve the problems we were wrestling with the night before.

Research has shown that a common cause of sleep disruption is a drop in blood-sugar levels in the night. A non-sugary snack before you go to bed may help. Bananas contain a natural sedative so try eating one about an hour before bedtime, and of course, short relaxation and breathing exercises are also helpful in getting us off to sleep in the first place.

## *Go to bed on a banana*

# EXERCISE

Applications for gym membership shoot up after Christmas and other periods of high indulgence, and just before the summer. But most of us know that regular exercise throughout the week, and the year, will be better for us than an occasional binge.

What if you haven't time to exercise? Either you have to take time to be healthy or you have to take time to be ill.

There are far too many exercise options to list here. Find something that suits you, and if possible find someone to do it with. The worry about letting the other person down might act as an added incentive to keep going. Schedule exercise into your diary, just as you do an evening out with friends.

## FUN

This can be a word to strike terror into the heart: 'Come on, it'll be fun. Don't be a spoilsport.' Enjoyment is a very personal commodity. Paintballing, tapestry, making model boats, Chinese cooking, learning ancient Greek and country dancing can all be great fun, but only if you enjoy them.

The important thing is to make time for some enjoyment, whatever it is. Research shows that becoming absorbed in something that we enjoy significantly reduces stress levels. In addition, laughter actually leads to a decrease in the amount of cortisol – the stress hormone – that we produce and improves the immune system.

# *Work to music*

Many 'fun' activities engage different parts of the brain to those that we use when working and so help our brain fitness. Listening to music, for example, involves both sides of the brain in processing melodies and rhythms. We may well produce better ideas after a session working on our favourite creative hobby than if we'd sat down thinking hard and seriously about it.

# ANSWERS

## Page 8–9 Warm-up

**1**  30

**2**  18 (Prime number + 1)

**3**  Tee, tea; two, too; whole, hole; scene, seen; banned, band; male, mail; vain, vein; tacked, tact

**4**  3

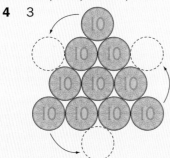

**5**  36 (tree = 9, flower = 6, vegetable = 10, fruit = 11)

**6**  MH

**7**  Mr Carpenter is a painter,
Mr Mason is a carpenter,
Mr Painter is a mason

**8**  Room 14 (Consonants = 1, vowels = 3)

**9**
| A | | | E F | | H I | |
|---|---|---|---|---|---|---|
| | B C D | | | G | | J |

**10**  TRIP 1: Cat to car – back empty-handed
TRIP 2: Roger to car – back with cat
TRIP 3: Sara to car – back empty-handed
TRIP 4: Cat to car

## Page 22–23 Limber up

A piece of cake: 3

All in the family: 5

Count on it:       7

Lost letters:      H, T, B, R
Country code:      10 (consonants = 2, vowels = 1)
Lucky 13:          TWELVE + ONE
Follow on:         18, 43 (+ 4, + 8, +4, +8 etc.)
Odd one out:       4 (August, January, March, Tuesday, July, September)

## Page 76 Test your semantic memory

Oslo, Ankara, Nairobi, Montevideo, Lhasa, Canberra, Riyadh, Bucharest, Sofia, Seoul, Damascus, Nicosia, Khartoum, Managua, Quito, Bogota, Bangkok, Caracas

## Page 99 What do you see?

Possible answers: a Mexican on a tightrope, necklace, fried egg on a line, stuffed olive on a skewer, tunnel, alien's eye

## Page 115–116

1  a) Please tell me your answer by Friday
   b) We are still short staffed
   c) We will not be able to do this for quite a while
   d) The suppliers did not give us an adequate reason for the delay
   e) We will have to find new ways to achieve our objectives
2  a) disinterested b) fewer c) formerly d) affect e) stationery
3  a) 7 out of 10 people can operate the new system
   b) I agree with some of Sue's points
   c) Please can you help me work out how much paper we'll need
   d) It's best to wait for George to be in a receptive mood
   e) I have a different idea

## Page 121 Daily workout plan

1  Use liquid to float it out; Suck it out (with or without a vacuum cleaner); Put a stick down with glue on the end
4  G, S, M (Game, Set and Match)
7  12 (It is not a prime number)

## Page 122 Analytical and logical thinking

1  44 (square = 13, circle = 8, triangle = 11, pentagon = 12)
2  STRANGE
3  Wz5, Yx3
4  D
5  Wine glass (not enough rings)
6  H = 1, P = 9, Q = 0
7  7 ways
8  6 + 7 + 8 + 9 = 30
   8 + 7 + 6 + 5 = 26
9  D

## Page 127 At least once a week

1   LASAGNE, GOULASH, MOUSSAKA, PAELLA, CURRY, HAMBURGER, OMELETTE, RAVIOLI, ENCHILADAS

2   1 down: XS, 2 down: LA

3   a) aromatic plant b) a duck c) a wood d) a dog e) cheese
f) animal that feeds on meat and vegetation g) semi-precious stone
h) used to pluck strings on a musical instrument i) sweet pepper

4   HEAD  HELD  HELL  TELL  TALL  TAIL

5   a) partridge/cartridge b) mortal/portal c) pine/mine d) minute/linnet)
e) garden/harden f) grand/spanned

6   a) INK b) ATE c) AND

7   potatoes, hooves, reefs, deer, allies, alleys, journeys, children, oxen, dances, princesses, audiences

8   bear/bare; made/maid; tied/tide; aid/aide; loan/lone; time/thyme;
ewe/yew; eight/ate; rhyme/rime; find/fined

9   handouts, freight, volley, unsliced, hustling, nectarines, cautioned, pictures, angrier, epitaphs, reduction, provides

10  box, duck, bear, right, pine, flat, grate, knot

## Page 130 Tone up your mathematical intelligence

1   91 (81 from the first 729, then 9 from the 81, then 1 from the 9)

2   40 (3 x 8 + 4 squared)

3   $23.43

4   D

5   45 litres

6   64

7   2400

8   18

9   ⅓ of 138

10  36 (5 + 1, 6 + 2, 8+ 4, 12 +8, 20 +16)
5  25 (2 2 squared, 3 3 squared, 4 4 squared, 5 5 squared)
46 (take away one less each time)

# RESOURCES

Kay Barwick, Liferoots:
The Hilltop Model, see page 113.

**Frames of Mind: The Theory of Multiple
Intelligences**
Howard Gardner, Basic Books, New York, 1983

**Emotional Intelligence: Why it Can Matter
More Than IQ**
Daniel Goleman, Bloomsbury, London, 1996

Taibi Kahler. Recipient of the 1977 Eric Berne
Memorial Scientific Award for his work on
miniscript and the five drivers.

**Time to Think: Listening to Ignite the Human
Mind**
Nancy Kline, Ward Lock, London, 1999

**Power up your Mind**
Bill Lucas, Nicholas Brealey, London, 2001

**Motivation and Personality**
Abraham Maslow, Harper and Row, New York,
1970

**SQ: Spiritual Intelligence, the Ultimate
Intelligence**
Danah Zohar and Ian Marshall, Bloomsbury,
London, 2000

## FURTHER INFORMATION

**The Thinking Environment**
Time to Think Inc.
UK: 63, Preston Crowmarsh, Wallingford,
Oxfordshire, OX10 6SL
US: 6004, Rhode Island Avenue, Riverdale, MD
20737
www.timetothink.com

**The Myers-Briggs Personality Type Indicator**
UK: Oxford Psychologists Press Ltd, Elsfield Hall,
15–17 Elsfield Way, Oxford OX2 8EP,
www.opp.co.uk
US: Consulting Psychologists Press Inc., 3808,
East Bayshore Road, Pao Alto, CA 94303,
ww.cpp-db.com

**Learning Styles**
UK: Peter Honey Learning, 10, Linden Avenue,
Maidenhead, Berkshire, SL6 6HB,
www.peterhoneylearning.com

## ACKNOWLEDGEMENTS

Executive Editor: **Trevor Davies**
Editor: **Rachel Lawrence**
Design Manager: **Tokiko Morishima**
Design: **Martin Topping at 'ome**
Illustrations: **David Beswick at 'ome**
Production Controller: **Jo Sim**

# INDEX